Contemporary

TENNIS

Contemporary

TENNIS

Roy Petty

cbi Contemporary Books, Inc.
Chicago

Library of Congress Cataloging in Publication Data

Petty, Roy.
    Contemporary tennis.

    Includes index.
    1. Tennis.   I. Title
GV995.P42   796.34'22   78-157
ISBN 0-8092-7548-1
ISBN 0-8092-7574-0 pbk.

Copyright © 1978 by Roy Petty
All rights reserved.
Published by Contemporary Books, Inc.
180 North Michigan Avenue, Chicago, Illinois 60601
Manufactured in the United States of America
Library of Congress Catalog Card Number: 78-157
International Standard Book Number: 0-8092-7548-1 (cloth)
                                    0-8092-7574-0 (paper)

Published simultaneously in Canada by
Beaverbooks
953 Dilligham Road
Pickering, Ontario L1W 1Z7
Canada

Contents

Introduction

In 1873, an Englishman named Major Walter Wingfield revived a 500-year-old French game, once called *jeu de paume* ("sport of the hands"), which consisted of hitting a ball back and forth over a seven-foot-high net with stringed wooden paddles. Major Wingfield called the game *sphairistike,* a Greek word. The name didn't catch on, but the game did: delighted players began to call it by the French verb meaning "play"—*tenez,* or tennis.

A year later, the game was brought to the United States. The first court in the country was set up on Staten Island, New York, and in 1881 the United States Lawn Tennis Association was established to standardize rules for the sport.

For generations, however, tennis remained largely a pursuit of the idle rich. Then, in the past decade or so, interest in the sport—probably sparked by the appearance of big-money pro tennis matches on television—boomed far beyond anyone's expectations. A decade ago there were an estimated 6 million tennis players in the United States; in 1976, there were at least 20 million, plus a projected 5 million more by 1980.

Tennis is a game of simple fundamentals. Ground strokes, serving, special strokes, and strategy—that's all there is to it. And most of it is far less difficult to learn than it appears at first, provided you learn the skills one step at a time, practicing and playing often.

This book has been set up to teach you the simple, basic movements of tennis—no gimmicks, no secret methods; just no-nonsense, step-by-step fundamentals. Master them, and you'll be playing winning tennis consistently in no time.

1

Equipment and courts

Some novice tennis buffs seem to think the only way to play a good game is to go to the nearest pro shop and load up with the most expensive and sophisticated equipment possible. That isn't at all necessary, unless you're an advanced player competing in tournaments regularly; a hard backhand and a consistent serve are worth more than all the $200 custom-made rackets in the world. On the other hand, you should know something about the equipment you'll be using on court. As your skills get better and better, the quality of your equipment will become more and more important.

Tennis racket

By far the most important piece of equipment in tennis is the racket. You don't have to spend a lot of money to get an adequate racket, but you do have to exercise some care in selecting the right racket for size and weight.

Tennis rackets are not all uniform. They vary in length, width, shape, size, and weight. Generally, though, the standard tennis racket is about 27 inches long and 9 inches at its widest point. It weighs between 12 and 15 ounces, without strings. (Figure 1.1)

The weight of most rackets is balanced right in the middle of the length—13½ inches from the butt end of the handle. However, many rackets balance at different points, meaning that the handle can be heavier or lighter than the head of the racket. Most players will choose an evenly balanced racket, but you might want to choose one that is a little unbalanced and tailored to the specific kind of game you play.

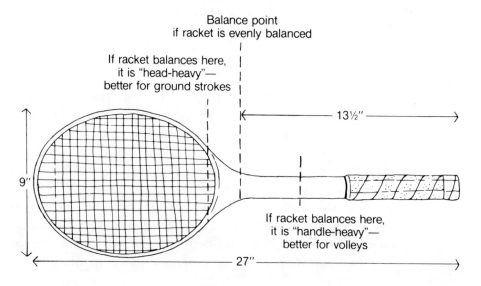

The Standard Racket

Figure 1.1

Here's a standard tennis racket. It is 27 inches long, and if the weight distributes equally halfway along its length—that is, 13½ inches from either end—it is considered "balanced," which is best for most players. "Head-heavy" rackets will balance closer to the strings, and are good for ground-game players; "handle-heavy" rackets will balance closer to the handle grip, and are good for volleyers.

A racket whose head is heavier than its handle will be most suitable for the player who spends most of his time in the back court, playing a hard groundstroke game. A head-heavy racket will allow you to have a smoother, more powerful stroke.

A racket whose head is lighter than its handle will be most suitable for the player who depends a great deal on his net game. The weight distribution lets you whip the racket around much faster than you could using a racket with a heavier head. And the power you could have with a heavier head isn't as important in a net game.

Your next concern should be the total weight of the racket and the size of the racket grip. The average (unstrung) racket for men should weigh between 13½ and 15 ounces, while for women it should weigh between 12 and 13¾ ounces—depending on what feels comfortable for them. Children should play with rackets weighing 12 to 13 ounces.

Racket grip size is measured by the circumference of the handle in inches. Some players feel comfortable with a relatively thick handle (usually recommended by tennis coaches), while others prefer thinner handles they can wrap their hands around more completely. Generally, men should use a grip measuring 4⅝ to 5 inches, while women should use a grip of 4½ to 5⅝ inches. Young children should use 4¼-to 4½-inch grips. Try different sizes out and see what feels best to you.

Wood or metal

The biggest debate in tennis sometimes seems to be whether wood or metal rackets are best—or whether there is any difference at all. For the beginning or intermediate player, this can be a bewildering debate.

Some teachers and coaches say wooden rackets give you better feel of the ball and absorb the shock of the hit, while metal rackets generally move more quickly and provide more power, but transmit the shock to your arm (this can be important if you're susceptible to tennis elbow).

Metal rackets are generally more expensive than comparable wooden rackets, but they last longer and require a bit less care than wooden rackets.

On the whole, the differences between metal and wood rackets may only be slight—and entirely negligible for the average recreational player. But if one kind feels better to you than another, then by all means choose the racket that is best for you.

A few tips on racket care: modern wooden rackets don't warp as easily as they used to, because of improvements in the lamination process (the best rackets will have as many as eleven thin slices of hardwood laminated together). However, to prevent warping, wooden rackets still should be kept in a racket press when they are in storage. Metal rackets do not require a press or any other special care. When you play, you won't be able to avoid occasionally scraping the racket against the ground, which can be hard on the exposed parts of the strings, looped around the edge of the racket face. To protect them, try putting a strip of adhesive tape around the edge of the racket head.

Strings: nylon or gut?

Most inexpensive rackets will already have been strung when they are sold. If you buy one and then decide to have it restrung later, or decide to buy a better-quality unstrung racket, you'll choose between nylon and gut strings (the latter made from strips of animal intestine.)

Most recreational players prefer nylon strings, simply because they're cheaper than gut, longer lasting, and less susceptible to damage. Gut strings are for the highly skilled player, who can take better advantage of the greater liveliness and better feel of gut strings. However, gut strings stretch and are adversely affected by moisture, so they must be replaced often. Since they cost about twice as much as nylon strings, and last half as long or less, it's worth thinking twice before buying gut. Nylon strings, by the way, also stretch out eventually and need to be replaced—as often as once a year if you play a lot.

The racket is usually strung at 50 to 70 pounds of pressure for gut strings, compared to 45 to 55 pounds for nylon. The greater the pressure, the livelier the racket will feel; but the strings will also wear out faster under increased pressure, and more shock will be transmitted to your arm and elbow.

If you buy gut strings, you'll also get a choice of gauge (thickness of strings). Standard thickness is 15-gauge. Tournament players will often choose the thinner 16-gauge strings, which are livelier but wear out even faster.

Tennis balls

Regulation tennis balls are about 2½ inches in diameter and weigh about two ounces. There are two kinds: championship and heavy-duty. Championship balls are best for grass or clay courts, while heavy-duty balls are best for hard courts.

Tennis balls aren't good if they don't bounce well, and their bouncing properties or liveliness depends on their freshness and exposure to air pressure. That's why new balls come sealed in vacuum cans. Regulation tennis balls, if dropped from a height of 100 inches, must bounce between 53 and 58 inches; any less than that, and they're considered too dead for tournament use. (Figure 1.2.) Tennis balls don't stay lively too long, whether they're being used or stored— even if they're stored still sealed in the vacuum can—so be sure you are using relatively fresh, new balls whenever you play. Dead balls make a rather slow and uninteresting game.

If you want to save a little money on balls, you can rejuvenate borderline balls by putting them through a regular cycle of your washer and dryer with a load of laundry. This will restore a bit of liveliness to them and fluff up the fuzz on the outside a little. If you play on hard courts, by the way, you'll wear out the balls much faster than if you play on grass or clay courts. Hard courts also quickly wear off the fuzz, which accounts for much of the weight of a tennis ball.

The "Bounce Test" for checking ball's liveliness

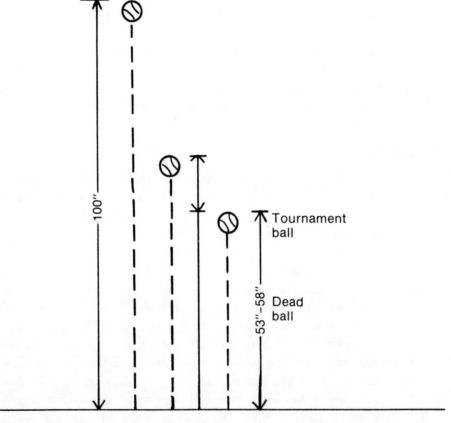

Figure 1.2

If you drop a tennis ball from a height of 100 inches, and it bounces less than 53 to 58 inches back up off the ground, it is considered "dead"—and you should buy fresh balls.

Shoes and other clothing

Good tennis shoes are more important than you might think. Tennis is hard on the feet, so be sure not to skimp on shoes. Get a pair to use especially for tennis that fit well, allow your skin to breathe—canvas is best—and provide maximum traction for the court surfaces you normally play on. A word of caution: some clubs with clay courts may prohibit you from wearing "basketball shoes" or sneakers with anything other than smooth-bottom soles. Shoes with deep ridges or traction patterns, acceptable for hard-surface courts, may be considered damaging for clay or other soft courts. Be prepared for that possibility.

For the rest of your tennis clothes, relatively loose-fitting shorts and T-shirts are the best, since they are the coolest and permit the best maneuverability. White is the traditional color for tennis clothes, and there's a reason for it: white reflects heat and can help keep you cooler than other colors during long matches. It is a good idea to wear a loose tennis hat or visor if the sun is overhead; sunglasses are absolutely not a good idea. If you wear glasses, get a head strap. Sweatbands on forehead and wrists are essential for some people, to keep sweat out of their eyes and off their hands, where it could loosen their grip on the racket. An etiquette tip for men: Some courts, particularly at private clubs, will require you to wear a shirt at all times. Be sure to take one along.

Court surfaces

There are three kinds of courts: grass, clay, and hard surfaces including asphalt or concrete, wood, and artificial surfaces. Each plays a bit differently from the others. (Figure 1.3)

GRASS COURTS. Rare in the United States, grass courts usually are seen only in tournaments or in very stodgy old tennis clubs, though they are more common in Europe and are, in fact, the traditional playing surfaces for the game (sometimes called lawn tennis). Balls bounce fast—which means they travel fast and far after bouncing—and relatively low on grass, and the surfaces can be uneven, meaning the ball can sometimes take strange bounces. Your feet will tend to slide on grass courts, too, no matter what kind of shoes you wear. On grass courts, the low, fast, uneven bouncing properties mean you'll want to emphasize your net game.

CLAY COURTS.   Again, clay courts are not as common in the United States as in Europe, but they are much more so than grass courts. Clay courts are by far the most common surface for tournaments. The ball bounces higher on clay than on grass, but much slower. This means the ground game is likely to predominate on clay, since it doesn't give the player much chance of rushing up to the net behind a booming serve or deep shot. Clay courts, too, tend to be uneven and cause unpredictable bounces. Both grass and clay courts have the disadvantage of requiring a great deal of

How balls will bounce on different surfaces

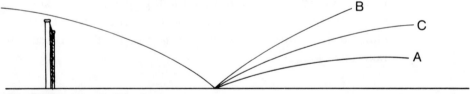

A—Grass: low and fast
B—Clay: high and slow
C—Hard surface (asphalt, concrete): high and very fast

Figure 1.3

Different court surfaces cause the ball to bounce different ways. Slowest court is clay; grass courts are next; and asphalt or other hard-surface courts are the fastest. Fast courts tend to emphasize net play, while slow courts tend to emphasize groundstroke play.

maintenance, as well as being unplayable for a long time after a rain.

HARD-SURFACE COURTS. Asphalt, concrete, wood, and artificial surfaces are all hard, smooth, and very fast, compared to grass and clay. Balls bounce faster than on grass, and higher, too, which means that your net game is likely to be more important than on clay surfaces—the harder the surface, the more likely you'll be able to get up to the net for volleying. Hard surfaces are uniformly smooth, and the ball won't take unexpected bounces. Asphalt and concrete are far more commonly used for courts in the United States than any other surface material (much more so than in Europe), because they require practically no maintenance. Occasionally you may run across wood surfaces or courts laid with hard but slightly springy artificial surfaces, such as those used on professional football or baseball fields. Such courts are almost always found in indoor tennis clubs, and they are likely to be even faster than asphalt or concrete. An added advantage of hard-surface courts is that your foot traction will be much better than on grass or clay. On the other hand, both balls and shoes wear out much faster on hard surfaces.

Photograph by Arthur Shay

2

The ground strokes: forehand

The forehand is the easiest of the basic tennis strokes to learn, and the one you'll probably use the most. But learning to do it right—for the greatest power, control, and consistency—takes a little study and practice. If you're just starting out in tennis, read this chapter carefully and practice your forehand often, paying special attention to the checklist at the end. Even good players sometimes let their forehands get sloppy, which can cost them points against more careful players. The forehand is the stroke which players will use for all deep shots that come to their right side and, for most players, also for shots that come straight at them.

(Note to left handers: This book has been written from the point of view of right-handed players. If you are left-handed, all the rules and pointers throughout the book apply to you, but with the hands reversed.)

The grip

There are three standard forehand grips: the eastern forehand, the continental, and the western forehand.

The eastern forehand is the most widely used and probably is the best for most beginning and intermediate players. (Figure 2.1.) For this grip, turn your racket on edge (the head perpendicular to the ground). With your hand outstretched, grasp the handle from the top so that the point of the V formed by your thumb and hand is directly over the top center of the racket handle. Contrary to what you may have heard elsewhere, you do *not* "shake hands" with the racket—the grip is similar to that, but not quite the same. The hand approaches the racket in the same position as if you were shaking hands, but the important point is that the racket handle is held mostly with the fingers, not with the full hand. If you truly "shake hands" with the racket, you'll be gripping it with your hand, which will not allow you full maneuverability. Instead, hold and control your racket mainly with your first two fingers and thumb, with the butt end of the racket resting right at the heel of the palm. Your

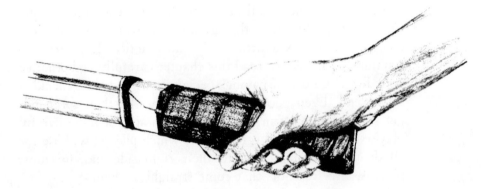

Figure 2.1

Eastern forehand grip: Place the "V" between thumb and fingers just to the right of top dead center on the racket handle.

index finger should be extended slightly, in a "trigger" position, for the best control. This grip gives you the best racket position for the straightforward return of a routine forehand shot, which usually comes in about waist high.

The continental grip is the kind used by advanced players, because it isn't necessary to change the grip for forehand or backhand shots. (Figure 2.2.) Unless your wrists are very quick and flexible, however, you won't want to depend on it at first. But try it once anyway. Grasp the racket so that the ball of your hand is directly over the top center of the handle; the V of your thumb and fingers should be slightly to the left of top center. Try this grip and then swing the racket out to your right side in position for a forehand shot. For most people, the racket face will assume a "closed" position—that is, the strings will be pointing slightly downward, instead of perpendicular to the ground.

Figure 2.2

Continental grip: Place the "V" of thumb and forefingers just to the left of top dead center of the racket handle. Don't "shake hands"—just hold the racket with the fingers, not the palm.

The western forehand grip is for players who like to put top spin on their forehand shots; it's a bit tricky for most recreational players. (Figure 2.3.) For this grip, grasp the handle directly from the right side so that the V of thumb and fingers is slightly to the right of top center on the handle; the thumb will be resting almost on top of the racket handle. Try this grip and swing the racket out into a forehand position; see how the racket face is in an "open" position (strings pointing slightly upward). If you swing your arm around in a natural follow-through, the racket face will tilt around from open to closed. This action, rolling from bottom to top during the stroke, is what gives the ball top spin, meaning it will bounce lower and faster in your opponent's court than a shot made with the racket straight ahead. However, you don't need to use a western grip to get top spin; any other grip can be used, without the drawback of putting top spin on every shot so that your opponent expects it.

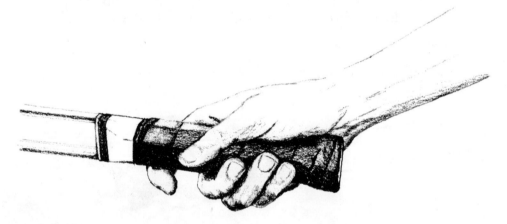

Figure 2.3

Western forehand grip: Place the "V" of thumb and fingers at the right corner of the top of the racket handle.

Whatever grip you use, be sure to grip the racket firmly enough so that the racket face will stay firm when it contacts the ball. Don't put a stranglehold on the racket or keep your wrist rigid, or you'll lose control and maneuverability, and your hand and wrist will get fatigued in a hurry.

The ready stance

Use this stance at all times when you're playing, no matter what kind of shot you're expecting. (Figure 2.4.) Hold the racket in front of you, with your elbow flexed so the racket is up a bit, almost head-high. Grasp the throat of the racket (just below the head) *lightly* with the fingers of your left hand, and assume a moderate crouching position—knees flexed, body bent slightly at the waist, feet about shoulder-width apart, and your body weight on the balls of your feet. From this position, you should be able to move in any direction with ease, and you should be able to pivot quickly on either foot.

Figure 2.4

In the ready stance, you should be prepared to move in any direction as quickly as possible. Keep your knees flexed slightly, feet shoulder-width apart, weight on the balls of your feet, and the racket held high, centered, and away from your body. The left hand is placed *lightly* on the racket throat, to help you change from forehand to backhand grip quickly.

Be sure your left hand is not holding the racket throat too tightly, or it could slow you down as you get into your backswing. The only reason your left hand is there is to help shift the racket for forehand or backhand grip position (we'll talk about the backhand grip in the next chapter).

The three-step forehand

The forehand shot has three basic phases: (1) pivot and step, (2) backswing, and (3) stroke and follow-through. These aren't really three separate, independent motions, however, but all parts of one smooth, fluid movement.

We'll go through it step by step, but remember that it should all be one smooth motion.

Step one: pivot and step

As soon as your opponent makes his serve or shot, you should recognize whether it will require you to make a forehand or backhand return, and get into position on the court to receive it. The proper forehand position is one in which the ball has bounced well in front of you and is coming to your right side, about four or five feet from your body. It is important to get into position right away, so you'll be ready to go into your backswing almost as soon as the ball passes over the net. If you're standing in position when the ball arrives, it will be much, much easier to make a good shot than if you are still running toward the ball.

When you're in position, pivot to the right on your right foot, stepping forward and around with your left foot. (Figures 2.5, 2.6.) In this position, your left shoulder should be pointed toward the net, your body facing the right side of the court, or even a bit farther away from the net. Your left foot should be a few inches or so ahead of your right foot, and your feet should generally be spread well apart, a little more than shoulder width.

It's important in the forehand stroke to pivot *toward* the ball, not away from it—that is, always pivot on your right

Figure 2.5

Forehand pivot: Turn your body to the right, with your weight on the right foot, and the racket held high and away from your body. Keep your eye on the ball.

Figure 2.6

Forehand step: Step around with your left foot so that your body is facing to the right side of the court, with the left foot slightly ahead of the right.

foot and step around with your left. If the ball is coming close to you, or right at you, don't try to pivot on your left foot and move your right foot back, because it will cause your body weight to shift in the wrong direction away from the ball instead of toward it. Half the power of the forehand stroke (or any stroke, for that matter) comes from the shift of the body weight into the ball. If a ball is coming too close to you, move back well ahead of time and then go into a normal forward step into the ball.

Step two: backswing

The biggest trouble beginners have with both forehand and backhand is getting the racket back in time. A smooth, unhurried backswing is critical to a good stroke. It takes a little practice, but you can quickly learn to watch the ball carefully when your opponent hits it; figure out whether you want to hit it forehand or backhand; get into the right court position; and go into your stroke—all by the time the ball crosses over the net. It sounds like quite a bit to do in a very short period of time, but after some practice and concentration, it will begin to come automatically.

Swing your racket straight back until your arm is extended away from your right side, as your body weight starts to shift onto your left foot. (Figure 2.7.) Be sure the racket goes straight back, not up high in the air or down low, or there's a chance you'll slam the ball into the net or pitch it up into the air. The best forehand stroke is straight back and straight forward again. Advanced players will often use a "loop" or "figure eight" backswing (Figure 2.8), in which the racket arm, in making the backswing, is swung up high and back around in a looping stroke. That's supposed to make the stroke more rhythmic, and it works for many players, but it isn't something you should try until you have become very comfortable with forehand shots.

A good way to gauge the flight of the ball and the

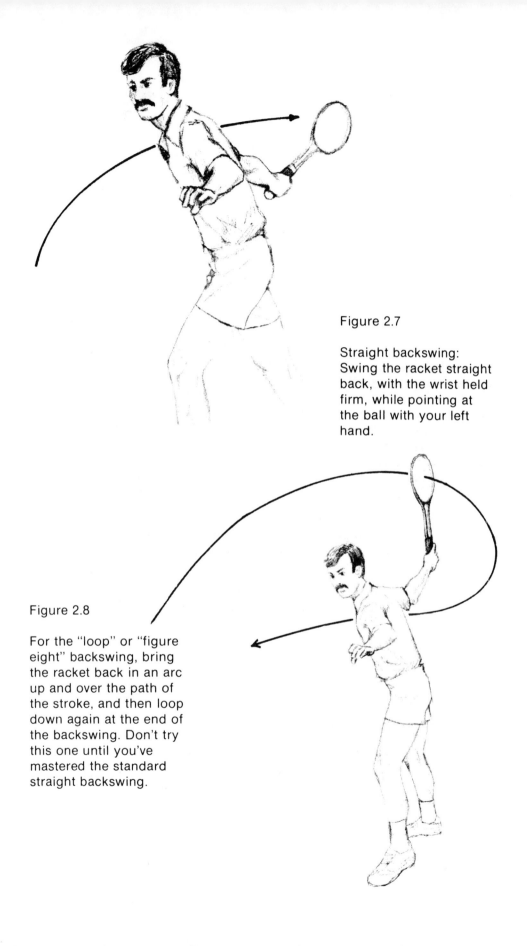

Figure 2.7

Straight backswing:
Swing the racket straight
back, with the wrist held
firm, while pointing at
the ball with your left
hand.

Figure 2.8

For the "loop" or "figure
eight" backswing, bring
the racket back in an arc
up and over the path of
the stroke, and then loop
down again at the end of
the backswing. Don't try
this one until you've
mastered the standard
straight backswing.

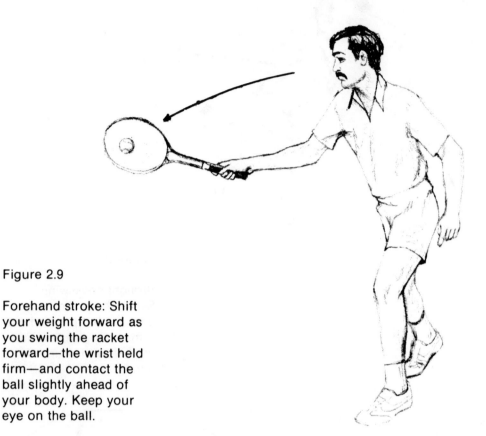

Figure 2.9

Forehand stroke: Shift
your weight forward as
you swing the racket
forward—the wrist held
firm—and contact the
ball slightly ahead of
your body. Keep your
eye on the ball.

timing of the stroke is to point at the ball with your left arm
when you go into the backswing—it will help your hand/eye
coordination. It isn't absolutely necessary; but you're not
doing anything with your left arm anyway other than trying
to keep it out of the way, so try it out.

Don't try to swing your racket back so far that you
strain your arm and shoulder. Such a swing isn't at all
necessary, and it only increases your chances of hitting the
ball much too hard.

Step three: stroke and follow-through

Stroke at the ball when it is well in front of you, so that
the racket will contact the ball in front of your body. The
best contact point is along an imaginary line 12 inches or so

20

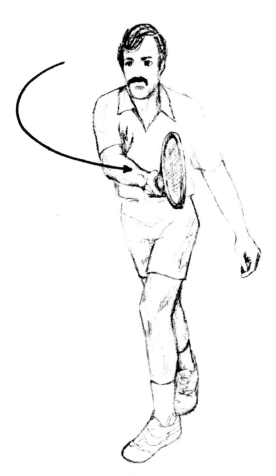

Figure 2.10

Forehand follow-through: After making contact with the ball, continue on around with a good follow-through, and keep it straight and level. The motion will twist your body around to face the net again, and you can return to the ready stance.

in front of your left foot; hitting the ball here will let you make the best use of your body-weight shift. (Figures 2.9, 2.10.) Don't let the ball get any farther back, or your arm will be behind your body and you'll lose the power of the stroke. Half the smoothness and power of the forehand comes from the shifting of the body weight forward, behind the racket arm and toward the net. Keep your wrist firm and relatively rigid in the stroke—don't swat at the ball.

Don't try to kill the ball, either. You will be surprised at how easy a stroke it takes to send a good, fast shot into your opponent's court. Making a smooth, accurate shot is better than trying to shoot a fireball back at your opponent. And whenever you try to take a hard slug at an ordinary forehand shot the chances are very high that it will go out of bounds. Save your smash shots for balls that bounce very high, where you're sure the angle of return is good and steep.

Don't hit *at* the ball; stroke *through* it. As in many other sports, the best way to hit a tennis ball is to swing through it as if it weren't there. The follow-through should be a smooth and continuous part of the stroke. Your follow-through should go all the way across your body, as the motion of the stroke carries you forward, and your right foot steps up, bringing you right back into the ready stance again.

The best time to hit the ball is when it has reached the height of its arc after the bounce. (Figure 2.11.) When the ball bounces in your court, it makes a smooth semicircular arc. At the top of that arc, not only is it as high as it's ever going to be, but it also is going more slowly and is easier to hit—good reasons to wait until that point, and no later, before trying to hit the ball. You want the greatest height possible for the forehand return, since the higher you stroke the ball, the faster and more accurate the shot can be. If you try to hit it too early or too late, when the ball is still coming up or starting to fall back down, you'll find it harder to judge

Hit the ball at the top of its bounce

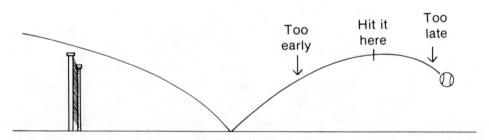

Figure 2.11

Hit ground stroke balls when they are at the top of their arc after the bounce—that's the point when the ball is at its highest position and slowest speed. "Early" or "late" hits are much more difficult to hit cleanly.

Figure 2.12

The WRONG way to hit a low return (above). Note that the back is bent, not the legs, and the player must "scoop" the ball with the racket head pointing downward. The ball will probably fly up in the air, presenting the opponent with a soft, easy return.

Figure 2.13

The RIGHT way to hit a low return (below). Bend at the knees as much as you have to, but keep the racket arm as level as possible, to avoid "scooping" the ball.

the height, and your chances of getting a solid hit in the center of the racket face are reduced.

Never, *never* bend down or drop your racket arm to stroke a low return. That's a sure-fire way to lob the ball up high in the air, meaning it will either go out of bounds or your opponent will smash it right down your throat. (Figure 2.12.) If your opponent sends a low return to you—and if he's any good at all, he'll try to do so as much as possible—bend at the knees as much as necessary to make the stroke. Keep the racket and racket arm as parallel to the ground as possible, making the stroke flat. (Figure 2.13.) If you don't, your tendency will be to scoop the ball up. The only time that's a good idea is when a well-placed shot by your opponent has thrown you completely off balance and put most of your court wide open for a "put-away" return. At such times, it can be valuable to lob the ball up slowly, to

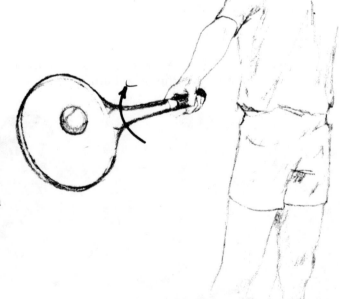

Figures 2.14, 2.15

Forehand top spin: Racket contacts ball in a slightly open position, and then the racket face is rotated *over* the ball through the stroke, as the wrist is rotated counterclockwise.

give you time to get back in position—but that's when you want to send the ball up *very* high, almost straight up. If you're planning on playing an opponent who likes to put top spin on his returns, you'd better practice going down low on your knees to make both forehand and backhand shots—top-spin shots will come at you much lower and faster after the bounce than those hit straight on.

Top spin and backspin

A word about spin: If you haven't mastered straightforward forehand shots to your satisfaction, you'd be better off not trying to complicate things by adding top spin or backspin to the ball. But many people find it quite easy to do, and

the ability to put spin on the return can be a very valuable tool for aggressive tennis players.

To put top spin on a forehand shot, make the three-step movement exactly as with a straight-on shot, but during the

How spinning balls bounce

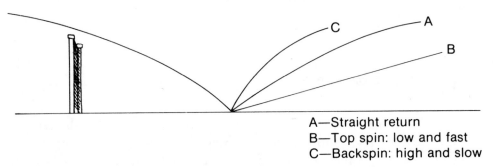

A—Straight return
B—Top spin: low and fast
C—Backspin: high and slow

Figure 2.16

Point A shows how a straight return, with no spin, will bounce in the court. B shows a topspin bounce—lower than normal, and usually faster. C is a backspin bounce—higher and slower, forcing the player to run up to the ball.

stroke, come at the ball with the racket "open" (facing slightly upward). At the point of contact, rotate your wrist counterclockwise smoothly through the stroke and follow-through. (Figures 2.14, 2.15.) You don't need to exaggerate the movement or do it jerkily to add spin to the ball. The wrist movement causes the racket to pick up the ball on contact and roll it over forward counterclockwise (as you face it). The ball flies normally until it bounces; after the bounce, it shoots forward unexpectedly low and fast. (Figure 2.16.) Many players try to hit most of their rally shots with top spin, although it's a good idea to vary the returns from straight-on to spinning—the way a pitcher mixes up fast balls and curves—to keep your opponent off balance.

Backspin is just the reverse. In the stroke, come at the ball with the racket face straight ahead, perpendicular to the ground. At the point of contact, rotate the wrist clockwise, rolling the ball backward—without scooping it—and bringing the stroke straight through the ball, despite the rolling action of the racket. (Figures 2.17, 2.18.) This motion will make the ball turn backwards and under. After it bounces, it makes a much shorter and higher arc than a normal straight-on hit. It is also much slower, which means it can be a setup shot for your opponent, if he is ready for it. Naturally, you won't want to use backspin very often—only as a change of pace when your opponent is expecting a long-bouncing hard return and is running backwards or waiting far back in the court.

Forehand checklist

The forehand is an easy, natural stroke for most tennis players—and it's easy to let it get sloppy. Practice this stroke as you would any other. If you can, have a friend watch you make forehand strokes from the sidelines. Ask him to rate you according to this checklist of the most critical or most-often-forgotten forehand points.

1. Are you moving into position as soon as your opponent swings his racket back?
2. Are you set in position when you start your backswing—not still running for the ball?
3. Are you starting your backswing by the time the ball crosses the net?

Contemporary tennis

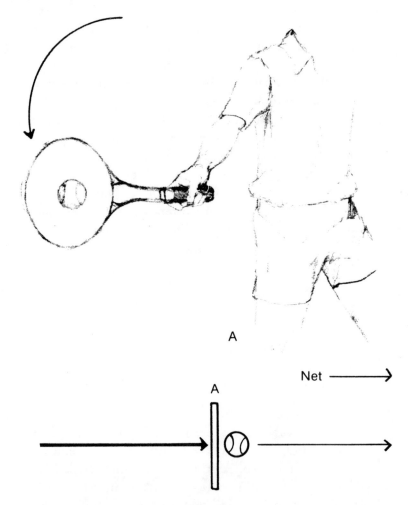

A

Net ⟶

A

Figures 2.17, 2.18

Forehand backspin: Racket contacts ball with face straight up and down, but rotates *under* the ball through the stroke as the wrist is rotated clockwise. Make the stroke straight and level—don't "scoop" the ball.

4. For low shots, are you bending at the knees and keeping your stroke level, instead of bending down at the waist?
5. Are you pivoting toward the ball—not away from it?

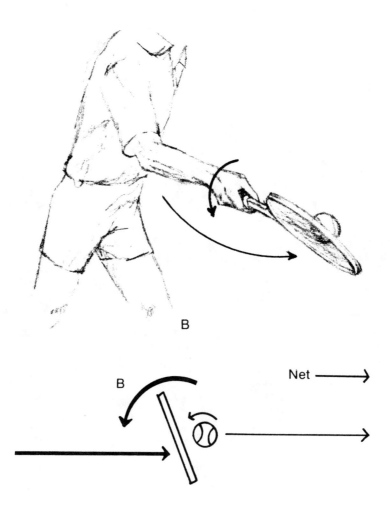

B

6. Is your racket making contact with the ball in front of your body?
7. Do you follow through smoothly, not hitting at the ball abruptly?
8. After the stroke, do you come back to the ready stance immediately?

Photograph by Arthur Shay

3

The ground strokes: backhand

The backhand stroke is the nemesis of many beginning players. The weaker your backhand is, the more you try to avoid using it; sharp opponents spot this weakness, and return more often to your backhand side. If you have a poor backhand, you've got two choices: keep racing across court to "run around" shots to your left side, thereby ensuring that you will never be a good player; or practice your backhand until you get it right.

Why does the backhand cause so much trouble for novices and even some intermediate players? It isn't an unnatural stroke at all; in fact, because of the way the shoulder and back are used, it can actually be a smoother stroke than the forehand. What seems to cause the trouble is not the shot itself, but the business of getting into the right position quickly enough. Once you learn to get into the backhand position quickly, so you can make a smooth, unhurried stroke, your difficulties should disappear; it may take a lot of practice, however. But advanced players often find that the backhand is their *best* stroke, believe it or not, and they may favor it over their forehand.

The grip

There are two basic backhand grips: the continental grip and the eastern backhand.

The continental grip, described in the preceding chapter, is a compromise between forehand and backhand grips, and it allows the player to hit either shot without changing his grip. (Figure 3.1.) That can be useful in fast, hard-hitting games, but it's a grip normally recommended only for advanced players who have learned how to maneuver their wrists and arms very quickly. Try it a few times anyway, to see how it feels. The continental grip, as described in the earlier chapter on the forehand, is one in which the hand is directly over the top of the racket handle (when the racket is set on edge, the strings perpendicular to the ground); the V of thumb and fingers should be slightly to the left of top center on the handle.

Figure 3.1

Continental grip: Place the "V" of thumb and fingers just to the left of top dead-center of the racket handle.

Figure 3.2

Eastern backhand grip: Place the "V" of thumb and fingers over the left corner of the top of the racket handle.

The most popular grip is the eastern backhand, largely because it seems to allow the player to put more power on the shot, even though there is the drawback that he must change the grip between forehand and backhand. (Figure 3.2.) For this grip, position your hand so the V of thumb and fingers is over the left edge of the racket handle; the ball of the hand will be slightly to the left of top center. Check the grip by swinging the racket across your body. The hand should be directly over the top of the racket handle, and the racket face should be perpendicular to the ground. Don't try to get your hand too far to the left side of the racket handle—it's too awkward to stroke the racket that way, and it's difficult to get into that grip quickly.

In the ready stance, as discussed earlier, you hold the racket straight out in front of you, with your left hand lightly gripping the throat of the racket. That left hand serves a purpose: to help you change your grip quickly, as soon as you see whether your opponent has hit you a forehand or backhand shot. The quickest way to change from a

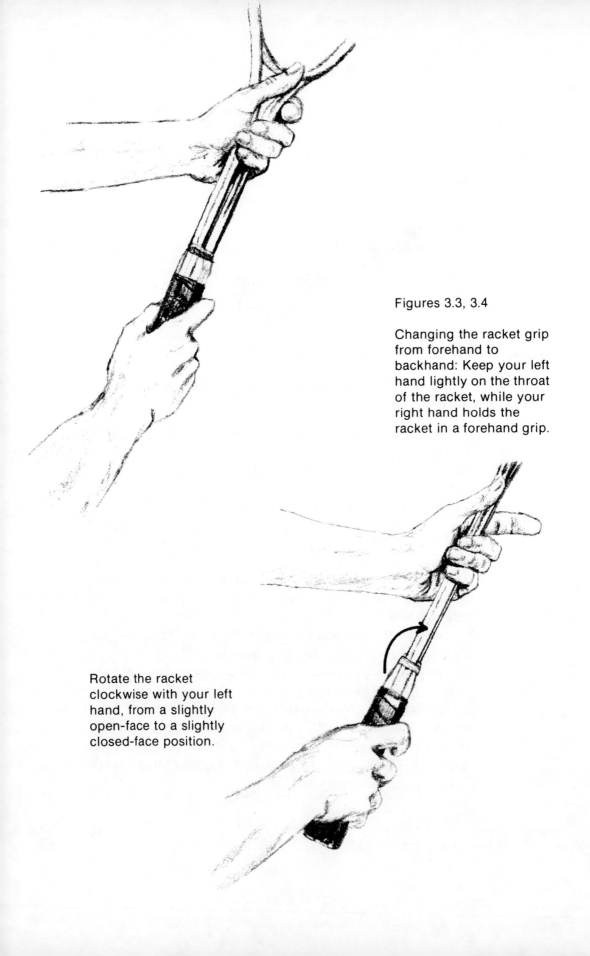

Figures 3.3, 3.4

Changing the racket grip from forehand to backhand: Keep your left hand lightly on the throat of the racket, while your right hand holds the racket in a forehand grip.

Rotate the racket clockwise with your left hand, from a slightly open-face to a slightly closed-face position.

forehand to a backhand grip is to keep the right hand in the same position, while with the left hand you rotate the racket clockwise (from your point of view) about 15 or 20 degrees, from straight up-and-down to a slightly "closed" position. (Figure 3.3, 3.4.) The racket grip then automatically changes from eastern forehand to eastern backhand. The reason for switching grips, by the way, is that as you move your right arm from the forehand position across your body to the backhand position, your arm will naturally rotate counter-clockwise—requiring a correction in racket position, in order to keep the racket face parallel to the ground.

The three-step backhand

The three phases of the backhand stroke are (1) pivot and step, (2) backswing, and (3) stroke and follow-through. As with the forehand, these are not three separate and distinct movements; they all blend together in one smooth motion.

Don't wait until you finish the pivot and step before you start your backswing, just because it's a different step in the movement. You should be in your backswing as you make the step, and the stroke forward should be a natural and uninter-rupted continuation of the whole motion.

Step one: pivot and step

Getting into position quickly, almost as soon as your opponent hits the ball, is even more important here than with the forehand. It's possible—though not desirable—to make a good running forehand shot, but it is much more difficult to do the same with a backhand shot.

As soon as your opponent hits the ball, and you see that it's going to require a backhand return, move into position, changing your grip for a backhand (don't look down at the racket handle to do so, however—keep your eye on the ball).

Figure 3.5

Backhand pivot: While changing your grip, turn your body well around and shift your weight to your left leg.

Figure 3.6

Backhand step: Step around with your right foot as you begin your backswing. Step all the way around—your back should be nearly facing the net.

(Figures 3.5, 3.6.) Pivot on your left foot, bringing your right leg around and forward until your right foot is well ahead of the left, both feet pointed toward the left side of the court, or even slightly away from the net.

You should pivot your body around farther for the backhand than you do for the forehand. In fact, you should have your back almost completely to the net, so that to keep your eye on the ball you must look over your right shoulder.

That's important. Many players fail to pivot far enough for the backhand, which means they strain the right arm awkwardly across the body for the backswing, losing both power and control. The farther you pivot, the easier the backswing and stroke.

Step two: backswing

Remember, don't wait until after you've pivoted and stepped to start the backswing. Blend the two together, so that a nice rhythm develops in motion.

Swing the racket straight back across your body; avoid the tendency to bring the racket up in an arc as you do so. That can cause you to "chop" at the ball, either slicing it badly or hitting it into the net. (Figure 3.7.) Don't strain to bring the racket as far back as your arm will go. If you need that much backswing, then you haven't turned far enough around.

Many players find that their backhand is smoother if they use the left hand to hold the racket throat lightly as they bring the racket back. It isn't necessary to the stroke, but you might find it useful, so try it a few times and see if it works for you. "Helping" the racket with the left hand during the backswing can both aid you in getting your racket back quickly and keep the racket steady for a smooth stroke. But be careful: You may find you have a tendency to grip the racket too tightly, or to "push" the racket into the stroke with the left hand, or even to turn the stroke into a two-handed backhand. You should avoid doing any of those things.

In the forehand stroke, you'll recall, the backswing is made with the racket arm relatively straight. That isn't necessary, nor always possible, with the backhand stroke. You will probably have to bend your racket arm moderately

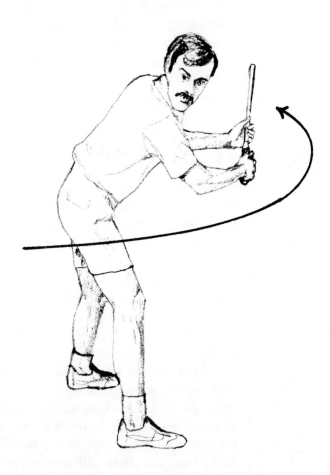

Figure 3.7

Backhand backswing: Take a good backswing, but avoid bending your arm too much, and don't strain too far. Keep your eye on the ball.

to get the racket back far enough for a good backswing. If you try to keep the arm straight, it will be awkward and uncomfortable, leading to an inaccurate hit.

Step three: stroke and follow-through

Make the stroke by bringing your arm straight around, unbending the arm as you do so, and shifting your weight smoothly onto your right foot. As with the forehand, you should keep the racket ahead of your body; so don't twist your body around with the stroke. Keep your back stationary.

Contact with the ball should come when your arm is straight out from your right side, slightly ahead of your body; and the follow-through should be a smooth continuation of the stroke movement. (Figures 3.8, 3.9.) There's a greater tendency in the backhand than in the forehand to "punch" at the ball; be alert to it and practice the follow-through carefully so you don't develop that bad habit. The follow-through will automatically cause you to rotate your body and bring your left foot around and forward, back into the ready stance again.

If you've watched much pro tennis, then you've probably seen players like Jimmy Connors and Chris Evert using a two-handed backhand stroke quite successfully. Beginning and intermediate players often try to develop a two-handed backhand, thinking that if it's good enough for Jimmy Connors, it should be good enough for them. One word of advice about using the two-handed backhand: Don't. Players of pro caliber are fast, strong, and experienced enough to modify their stroke styles unconventionally and get away with it. For the rest of us with lesser skill, a two-handed backhand is awkward and terribly inaccurate, and trying to learn it can actually impede your learning a conventional backhand properly.

Figure 3.8

Backhand stroke (left): Contact the ball just ahead of your body. Be careful that you don't get too close to the ball in the backhand; if this happens, you'll have to make your stroke with your arm bent, and you'll lose power and accuracy.

Figure 3.9

Backhand follow-through (below): Keep your follow-through level—don't inadvertently swoop your racket up into the air. Let the follow-through carry you on back around into the ready stance.

Backhand checklist

The best way to master the backhand is to practice, practice, practice. Find a friend who wants to practice ground strokes and spend one or two sessions a week simply hitting backhands to each other. An even better way to practice the backhand is to have your friend hit an assortment of backhand and forehand shots to you, so you'll have to wait in the ready stance, ready to pivot left or right for either stroke. That's an excellent way of learning to get into position far enough and fast enough for a good backhand, with the added bonus of getting in some forehand practice as well.

If you practice the backhand long enough, you may discover to your amazement that it is an easier stroke for you than the forehand. The back, shoulder, and upper arm muscles used in the backhand stroke are usually stronger than those used in the forehand. Once you master the form of the stroke, you may find that the backhand is smoother and more accurate for you than the forehand.

Get a second friend to stand at the left side of the court and watch you hit a few backhand strokes. Ask your friend to rate you according to this checklist:

1. Are you starting to pivot and begin the backswing before the ball crosses the net?
2. Did you change your grip?
3. Did you pivot toward the ball properly, or away from it?
4. Is your back turned to the net as you complete the pivot and step?
5. Are you keeping your eye on the ball over your right shoulder?
6. Do you avoid pulling your racket up during the backswing as it crosses your body?
7. Do you avoid twisting your body around during the stroke?
8. Do you make a complete follow-through, hitting through the ball instead of at it?

Photograph by Arthur Shay

4

The serve

There's no getting around it: serving is half the game of tennis. Master a fast, accurate, consistent serve, and you'll always be a competitive player. On the other hand, if your service is weak and inconsistent, you'll be severely handicapped no matter how good your ground game or net game is.

The key to a good serve is remembering that it's a great deal like throwing a baseball. Try it. Pick up a tennis ball and make a good, ordinary overhand throw. Now, imagine as you throw that you have a tennis racket instead of a baseball in your hand; that motion, essentially, is the one you'll want on the tennis court. A "windup," or backswing; contact with the ball when your arm is fully extended above your head, right where you would release the ball in a baseball throw; and a smooth follow-through—that's the heart of a good serve.

But let's go through it step by step.

Foot position

Start by placing your left foot (if you're right-handed) a few inches behind the back-court line, at a 45-degree angle to the line. (Figure 4.1.) Put your right foot about 18 inches or so, about shoulder width, behind your left foot, parallel to the base line. Adjust your feet so that your left shoulder is pointing down an imaginary line to the center of the court you'll be serving into; your body should be facing perpendicular to that line.

During the serve, you'll be shifting your weight from foot to foot, starting with your front foot, then the back foot, then the front foot again. You won't be moving your feet very much—in fact, you don't have to move your feet at all to have a powerful serve, contrary to what you might think. But you might take a short step forward, so be sure in placing your feet before the serve that you're far enough back from the line that you won't commit a "foot fault." If you're not sure about it, have a friend watch you serve a few times to see how much you're moving your feet forward and whether you're stepping over the line.

Figure 4.1

Serving foot position: Front foot is at a 45-degree angle to the net, at least several inches away from the baseline. Back foot is parallel to the net. Feet are about shoulder-width apart.

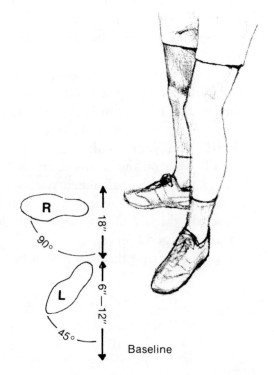

Baseline

The grip

For a flat, hard serve, grip the racket the same way you would for a forehand shot. Set the racket on edge and grasp it with your fingers from the right-hand side. Check the grip by swinging the racket up and around in a service motion. When your arm is straight up and fully extended, the racket face should be perpendicular to that imaginary line drawn into the serving court. That's important; adjust your grip accordingly.

For a spinning serve, move your grip so the hand is more directly over the top of the racket handle. The idea here is to have the racket face turned so it will contact the ball on the left side and roll it around to the right as you serve. That gives it the spin that makes it hard to receive.

Remember to keep the grip fairly firm, but not too tense. If your grip is too rigid, you won't be able to hit the ball accurately. If it's too loose, you'll hear a weak thud when the ball contacts the racket, and there won't be any power in the stroke at all.

The three-step serve

Basically, there are three steps in the serving motion: (1) the windup and toss, (2) the backswing, and (3) the stroke and follow-through.

When you can put these three steps into play with one smooth, easy motion, you'll have a deadly serve.

Step one: windup and toss

Get into your stance and point the racket head toward the serving court, about waist-high. Extend your left hand, holding the tennis ball loosely in the fingers, out to the throat of the racket. Keep your arms and body loose and relaxed.

Then, in one smooth motion, swing the racket straight back in a low arc while the left hand drops a bit and then

Figures 4.2, 4.3, 4.4

Windup and toss: Start with racket arm partially extended and pointing toward the serving court; hold the ball with the left hand at the racket face. Drop both hands at once, the racket arm going into a low swing back while the left hand drops straight down.

tosses the ball up, releasing it about shoulder height. (Figures 4.2–4.4.)

The toss is extremely important—in fact, it's the most troublesome part of the serve for most beginners. You should practice your toss until it becomes consistent; you want to place the ball right where the center of the racket face will hit it every time.

46

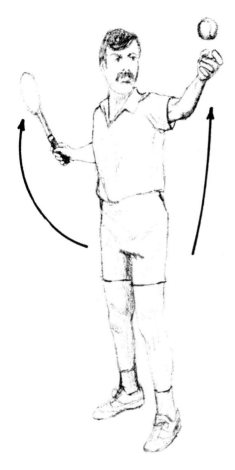

The left hand then goes straight back up for the ball release. Release the ball at shoulder-to-head height, when the racket is straight back behind you.

A good toss should go straight up from where you release it to exactly as high as the racket face, when your right arm is fully extended above your head. When you toss the ball straight up, notice that point at which the ball stops going *up* and starts to go *down* again—it seems to hang there for a split second, just waiting for your racket to smack it across the court. For a moment, the ball is motionless in the air, and that's the best time to hit it. If you try to hit the ball

47

when it is still flying up or when it's falling back down, your chances of hitting it accurately and solidly, right in the center of the racket face, are greatly reduced.

Check the height of your toss by holding your racket fully extended over your head, and tossing the ball straight up from your partially extended left arm. The toss should go exactly as high as the racket face, and then fall right back down into your hand again. Remember, toss the ball *straight up*, not in a big arc—you don't want to be chasing it with your racket in the middle of the serve.

The height of the toss is critical. Toss it too high, and the rhythm of the serve will be thrown off, since you'll be waiting for the ball to come back down to serving height— and you'll be much less likely to hit it solidly anyway. Toss it too low, and you'll have to bend your racket arm to hit it, reducing the power of the serve and the angle of its flight into the opponent's serving court.

Step two: backswing

For the backswing, it helps to remember your baseball throw. You get the power in your throw from the windup, in which you swing your arm back behind you in a circular motion until the elbow is fully "cocked," the ball behind your shoulder. Put a tennis racket in your hand, and the motion is the same. At the point your elbow is bent, ready for the stroke, the racket should be pointed straight down your back. (Figures 4.5, 4.6.) The power comes from this motion, as does the rhythm of the serve. The backswing should be timed just right, so that your elbow is fully "cocked," with the racket pointing almost straight down behind your back, just as the ball is reaching the top of the toss, at serving height.

Practice the first two steps of the serve frequently. Wind up and toss the ball, then go into your backswing, and stop. Right when you stop, your left arm should be up at

Figures 4.5, 4.6

Backswing: After ball release, swing racket all the way around behind your back, with the arm cocked. Side view shows how racket should be pointing straight down your back for the most power.

shoulder height, having just tossed the ball. The ball should be almost at serving height, and your racket should be pointing down your back, ready to uncork the stroke.

Don't strain, and don't try to kill the ball. The power of the serve comes from the backswing and the smoothness of the stroke, not from how hard you grunt and strain to whack the ball—you need to stay loose and relaxed, or your serve

49

will never be accurate. You can deliver a very hard and fast serve without working at it much at all. If you're all worn out after you practice half a dozen serves, then you're straining too hard.

Step three: stroke and follow-through

Practice that baseball throw again. After the windup, note how your body shifts forward as the throwing arm comes up and out. The ball is released just a bit past the point where your arm is straight up in the air, and you should have a smooth follow-through. Do it the same way with your tennis racket: one smooth, circular motion, vertical to the ground. (Figures 4.7, 4.8.)

There are some differences from that fast-ball pitch, however. First, you don't take a big step forward as you shift your weight for the stroke. You don't want to move your left foot at all, in fact. Second, you should keep your eye on the ball all the way through the serve.

At the moment the racket face contacts the ball, your body should be fully extended, with your body weight on your left foot. At contact, the racket shouldn't be exactly vertical, or the ball will go sailing straight out of bounds. Instead, hit it just a few degrees past vertical, at a slightly downward angle, so the ball will be aimed straight toward the serving court.

Swing smoothly through the ball; don't hit at it. And allow your follow-through to be a smooth continuation of the stroke motion. If your stroke is choppy, your accuracy and power will be reduced. Make sure the follow-through is straight down across your body, and not swooping off to one side or the other.

Remember, at the point of contact, your body and racket arm should be fully extended, for the best results. If your stroke is made with the racket arm bent slightly, you'll lose some of the smoothness of the stroke. Most important,

Figures 4.7, 4.8

Stroke and follow-through:
Swing straight overhand as
the ball reaches racket height;
the motion is similar to
pitching a baseball. Contact
the ball over your right
shoulder, a little ahead of your
body. Keep your eye on the
ball. Then follow through
smoothly—hit *through* the
ball, not *at* it—and avoid
stepping forward over the
baseline with your right foot.

Figure 4.9

A too-low toss will require you to bend your racket arm in order to hit the ball, meaning you'll lose power and accuracy, and the angle of the serve into the opponent's court will be reduced.

Figure 4.10

A too-high toss means you'll be stretching or jumping at the ball, losing all the power of your body—and chances are, the serve will be inaccurate.

Figure 4.11

If you try to hit the ball too far forward, two things will probably happen: first, you'll hit the ball into the net, since the racket will strike the ball at too much of a downward angle; and second, the throwing of your weight so far forward to reach the ball will probably cause you to commit a foot fault.

you'll lose height. (Figure 4.9.) The higher in the air you hit the ball, the better the angle into your opponent's court— and the more accurate your serve can be. On the other hand, if you try to hit the ball *too* high, you'll find yourself reaching up on tiptoes or, worse, jumping at the ball. (Figure 4.10.) In either case, you're likely to lose your balance and foul up the serve; and if you jump into the air, you'll lose all the power of the windup and backswing.

If you try to hit the ball too far forward, well ahead of your body, you will either hit the ball into the net or commit a foot fault. (Figure 4.11.) If you try to hit the ball too far back (directly above your head or slightly behind that point), your serve will probably sail over your opponent's service line. These errors are an indication that your toss is not accurate. Practice it.

Better yet, remember that when you're serving in a game, you can toss the ball up as many times as you want, as long as you don't swing. The minute you swing, it's a serve; but if you toss the ball up and don't swing, it doesn't count as a serve. That way, if in the early part of your serve you realize your toss was no good (too far forward or back, too low or too high)—keep your racket down, stop the serve, catch the ball with your left hand, and start all over.

Spin and slice serves

Once you've mastered the basic flat serve, you should practice a top-spin or slicing serve. Either one is a bit tricky to learn, but both can be an important part of your repertoire—to go back to the baseball analogy, it's like a pitcher's knowing how to throw both a fast ball and a curve. You can keep your opponent on his toes by varying the serves you make. Most advanced players, in fact, tend to use top-spin serves more than any other. Putting top spin on a serve makes the ball travel a bit slower and higher than with a hard flat serve, but the ball will bounce low and fast, often slightly to your opponent's left, making it harder for your opponent to guess where to make his return.

To add top spin to your serve, you'll have to change both your starting position and your toss. First, place your feet and your body so that you're facing more directly parallel to the base line, a bit farther around than for a standard flat serve. You should have to look down along the line of your left shoulder to see your opponent. Next, start

Figure 4.12

Start out a topspin serve by
holding the racket and ball to
the right of your body, instead
of directly in front of it.

your windup normally but toss the ball up farther to the
right of your body than usual. Your tossing arm, instead of
pointing toward the net, should be pointing generally parallel
to the base line. (Figure 4.12.) Make the backswing normally,
but make the stroke in a big diagonal curve out to the right
of your body to meet the ball. You should rotate your wrist
and racket in a clockwise direction as you meet the ball.
(Figure 4.13.) Your arm should be almost fully extended for
the stroke, but not quite as high as for a flat serve, since at
the point of contact you'll have to extend the racket even a
bit farther, across and over the ball (Figure 4.14.) The point
here is to contact the ball from the lower left-hand side with
the racket and "roll" it up and around to the upper right-
hand side, with the end of the stroke and follow-through
coming back across your body.

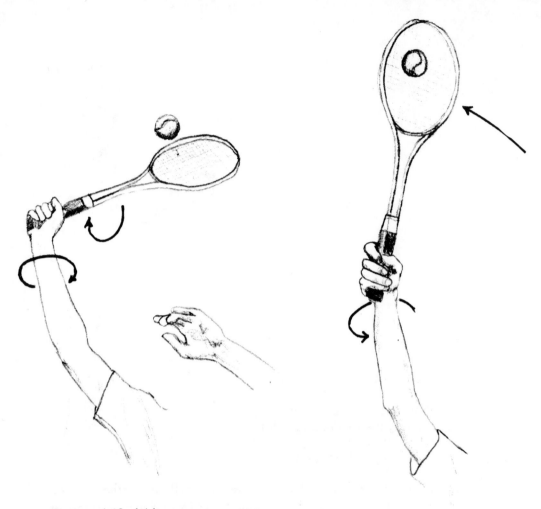

Figures 4.13, 4.14

The topspin serve: You should try to rotate the racket face over the top of the ball as you contact it in the stroke. Do this by making contact on the lower side of the ball, rolling the ball upwards with the racket as you rotate your wrist slightly clockwise.

It sounds complicated, but many players find the top spin relatively easy to learn, once they have mastered the trick of rotating their wrist enough during the contact portion of the stroke. Once you've got a basic top-spin serve down pat, practice trying to exaggerate the twisting motion even more, rotating not just the wrist but the whole arm as well—that's the deadly "American twist" serve, the hardest

Figure 4.15

Slice serve: Hit the ball straight through during the stroke, but make contact with the racket face turned a little to the left; the wrist should be turned clockwise a few degrees when you hit the ball. Be careful that you don't *roll* the ball upwards, or the serve will turn into a weak topspin serve.

serve of all to return. It bounces low, fast, and sharply off to the opponent's left.

Another variation is the slice serve. For this one, make a standard flat serving motion, but hold the racket in a backhand grip so that at the point of contact the racket face will be turned somewhat upward to the left, rather than pointing straight at the net. (Figure 4.15.) This serve will be very soft, but it can surprise your opponent by traveling much farther off to your opponent's right than he expects. Be sure when you hit the ball that the direction of the stroke is more to the right than for a normal flat serve, since you don't want to hit the ball out of bounds to the left. You shouldn't use this serve very often, but it's a good change of pace to keep your

How different serves bounce

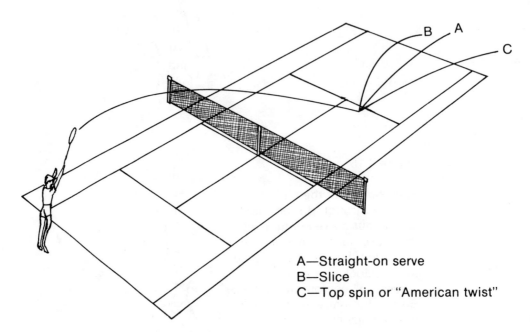

A—Straight-on serve
B—Slice
C—Top spin or "American twist"

Figure 4.16

A slice serve (B) will bounce off to the left of a straight-on serve (A); a topspin or "American twist" serve will shoot off lower than a straight serve, and generally off to the right.

opponent alert—and maybe give you an occasional "ace" point. (Figure 4.16.)

Vary your serves. Remember, for every point you have two serving opportunities, so don't be afraid to take a chance on a hard first serve or a top-spin serve. If you fault the first serve, you can make a somewhat safer second serve. On the other hand, don't make the common mistake of always trying to destroy the ball on the first serve, with little hope of actually hitting a good one. You'll find yourself in the position of always having to hit a soft, safe second serve or risk double-faulting. Once your opponent figures that out, he'll learn how to handle your second serve, and you will find out how unsafe a "safe" serve can really be. Always try to make the first serve good. Try a flat serve one time, and a spinning serve the next. Don't be predictable, or you'll lose the precious advantage of the serve and set yourself up for a devastating return and a needlessly lost point.

Practicing your serve

More than any other single part of your game, your serve needs continual practice—and unless you've got a court in your backyard or otherwise have regular and easy access to a court, it may not be a simple matter to get that practice. Unlike some other strokes, you can't adequately practice your serve anywhere but on a tennis court. If you live in an area where court time is hard to come by, you might try finding a friend who also wants to practice his serve, and the two of you can take an hour of practice every now and then, standing on opposite sides of the net and serving into each other's empty court. Bring a sackful of dead balls and keep serving until they're all gone, then switch sides or gather up your partner's spent balls and start all over. Start your practice serves off slowly; hit very gentle, straight-on serves, practicing only the form at first, until you can comfortably add a little power and perhaps a few gimmicks, such as different kinds of spin, to the serve.

You might also find it useful to practice just the first step in the serving motion—the windup and toss—repeatedly until you can do it uniformly every time. That is something you *can* practice in your own backyard. Perform just the first half of the serve, from windup, to toss, to backswing—and stop there and do it over. The point of this is to learn to toss the ball into exactly the right height and position, and to have your arm and shoulder poised exactly right, so that you can do it the same way every time literally without thinking about it. (Figure 4.17.)

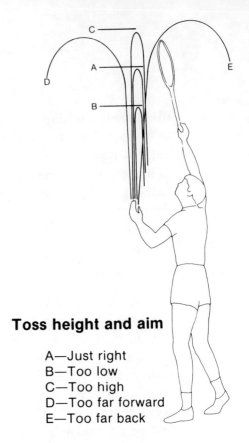

Figure 4.17

Practice your toss as often as
possible. Hold the racket
straight over your head and
toss the ball with your left
hand; a good toss will go
straight up and down,
reaching its highest point
right at the level of your racket
face—that's when it will be
momentarily motionless, and
will be hit most easily.

Toss height and aim

A—Just right
B—Too low
C—Too high
D—Too far forward
E—Too far back

It's also extremely valuable to have a friend (someone
who knows something about tennis) watch your serve from
the side of the court. Give him the checklist at the end of this
chapter and have him concentrate on a single item in each
serve. If you really are serious about perfecting your serve,
have your friend take photographs of you as you make your
serve—two or three pictures of each phase of the serve, from
windup to follow-through (though the serving stroke itself
will probably be blurred)—so you can examine your own
form from the prints later on. It isn't as far-fetched or useless
an idea as it might sound; try it once.

Serving checklist

Have your friend go through this checklist, item by
item, as he's watching you practice your serve. Unless you're
already an advanced player, you'll probably make one or
more mistakes in each serve. Don't let it bother you. Instead,

draw up a checklist of your own weak spots for extra concentration, and work on those until it all becomes second nature to you.

1. Is your racket grip right—does it permit the racket face to be pointing directly at the net at the top of your stroke?
2. Are you standing far enough back of the line to avoid committing a foot fault?
3. Is your weight mostly on your left (forward) foot as you begin your serve?
4. Are you releasing the toss just as your racket arm reaches the point farthest back in the windup position?
5. Are you releasing the toss from a high enough position (no lower than shoulder height)?
6. Is the toss high enough? Is it straight up and down? Is it in the right position for the stroke (not too far in front nor too close to your body)?
7. Is your eye on the ball at all times?
8. Is your backswing directly behind you—does the racket point down your back?
9. Are you shifting your weight forward to your left leg for the stroke?
10. Are your racket arm and your body fully extended as you contact the ball?
11. Are you meeting the ball properly, at a slightly downward angle, slightly ahead of your body?
12. Are both feet (especially your left foot) on the ground during the stroke—you're not leaping into the air?
13. Is your stroke smooth and easy? Are you sure you're not trying to kill the ball?
14. Is your follow-through complete and smooth, as if you were hitting through the ball?
15. Is your weight still well balanced as you complete the serve? Good balance is a sign of a proper serve (and a safeguard against foot faults).

5

Volley, lob, and smash

A good, competitive tennis player needs to have more than just skillful ground strokes in his repertoire. He should also know how to make three special kinds of shots—the lob, volley, and smash—which are essential to an aggressive tennis game. They are easy to learn, compared to the ground strokes; but it requires considerable skill to learn how and when to use them properly.

This chapter tells what they are and how they are used, and then discusses how to make each of the three special shots. (Figure 5.1.)

Volleying is an indispensable part of any good tennis game. A volley is the return of any ball before it bounces. Volleys are hit from much closer to the net than the ground strokes, and they enable the player to get the ball back to his opponent much more quickly than he could with a ground stroke. If you are able to move up close to the net and volley your opponent's shots back at him, you have put him at a

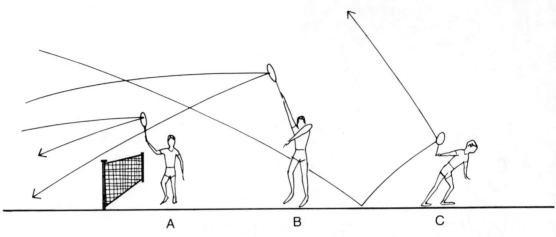

A—Volley
B—Smash
C—Lob

Figure 5.1

Stay close to the net for volleying and hit the ball before it bounces, preferably forcing it downward. For the smash, hit the ball strongly downward in a straight overhead swing—just like a serving stroke motion. For the lob, wait until the ball bounces and hit it very high up into the air.

very serious disadvantage. You can place your shots wherever you want, and you can return shots so quickly that your opponent will be constantly on the defensive.

The lob is both an offensive and a defensive shot. It consists of nothing more than scooping the ball up deliberately and sending a very high, slow shot over the net. It is most often used defensively, when your opponent's shot has caught you off balance and out of position—when your situation provides a setup for him to return the ball to a far corner, where you can't get to it in time. In cases like that, you may have to lob the ball high up into the air. The only purpose of the defensive lob is to keep the ball floating up in the air, out of your opponent's reach, long enough for you to recover and get back into good court position—in this case, ready for the smash he will no doubt try to send you. An offensive lob isn't used very often, but it can be extremely effective once in a while. It is, in fact, an excellent way of keeping your opponent from rushing to the net for a volleying game. When your opponent hits a long, low "approach shot" (meaning a shot that gives him the time and opportunity to run up to the net) and dashes forward, you can throw him off balance by hitting a high, deep lob. He would be able to volley back a return at normal height, but for a lob over his head he'll have to stop his net approach and run backward to catch the ball.

The overhead smash is the weapon you use to "put away" a weak ball or a high-bouncing lob from your opponent. When your opponent has hit a high shot to you, you can get underneath it and give it a very hard overhand hit into a corner where he can't reach it, for an easy and demoralizing point. The only problem with the smash is that many players try to use it too often and under the wrong circumstances, cleverly smashing the ball straight out of bounds—an embarrassment and a wasted point for the over-anxious player.

The volley

When a ball is hit into your court, it carries with it a considerable amount of energy. Unfortunately, much of that energy is lost when the ball bounces, and it slows down. That's why ground strokes require a full backswing, weight-shifting body movement, and complete follow-through to get a solid return over the net.

In volleying, there isn't time to make a full backswing and stroking motion. Fortunately, it isn't necessary. The ball carries enough energy with it before the bounce that all you have to do is put the racket face in front of it, and it will return easily back over the net.

Consequently, the stroke for both forehand and backhand volleys is very short and doesn't require much power. And if you're playing right at the net (as occurs most commonly in doubles), you don't have to make a stroke at all. You can just block the shot with your racket.

Because you must get your racket into position much more quickly than for bouncing ground strokes, you will have to make volley strokes without pivoting very far around. The forehand volley is made with the body almost directly facing the net, and the backhand volley with the body turned, at most, to a point 90 degrees to the net—only enough to reach the ball without having your arm cross your body awkwardly.

For the forehand volley, get into the ready stance and stay alert, your weight on the balls of your feet, your knees flexed, and your racket up high. (Figures 5.2, 5.3.) Pivot on both feet quickly to the right, and step around with your left foot only if necessary to reach the ball. Don't make a backswing at all; just get your racket up and take a sharp, quick swing at the ball—but don't try to put too much power into it. Be sure to keep your eye on the ball. After the hit, get back into the ready stance immediately.

For the backhand volley, pivot quickly to the left and make a quick step around with your right foot. You'll almost always have to step around for the backhand volley, much more often than for the forehand. (Figures 5.4, 5.5) Get your racket up high quickly and try to take as little backswing as possible. Simply make a sharp stroke and get back into the ready stance.

Remember to check your grip when you're volleying, and watch the position of the racket face. The idea in volleying is to hit the ball down at a relatively steep angle, into a corner or past your opponent. If the racket face is pointing up to the sky, you've wasted the advantage of the volley and put yourself in a very precarious situation for the return. If the racket face is pointing too far down, the ball could go right into the net.

Since you may not have time to change from forehand to backhand grip during volleying, you may want to use a continental grip so you can play both forehands and backhands without changing your grip.

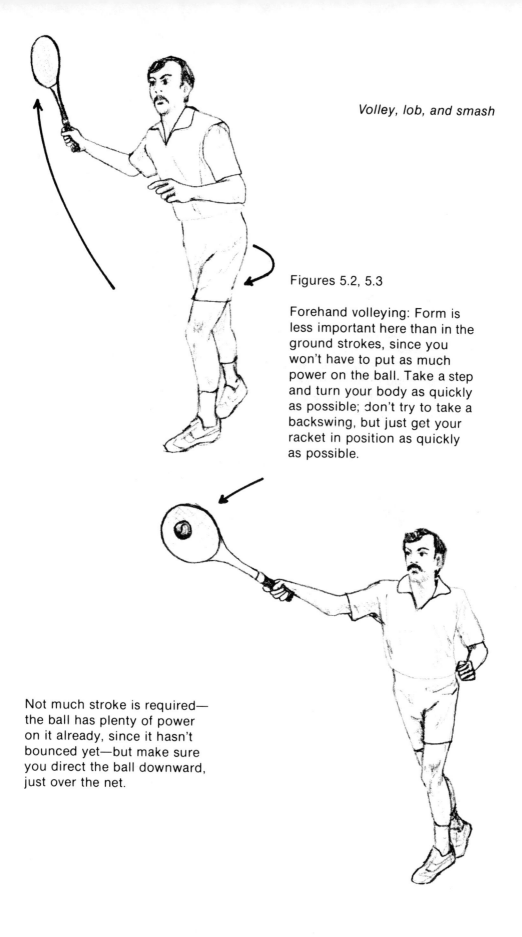

Volley, lob, and smash

Figures 5.2, 5.3

Forehand volleying: Form is less important here than in the ground strokes, since you won't have to put as much power on the ball. Take a step and turn your body as quickly as possible; don't try to take a backswing, but just get your racket in position as quickly as possible.

Not much stroke is required— the ball has plenty of power on it already, since it hasn't bounced yet—but make sure you direct the ball downward, just over the net.

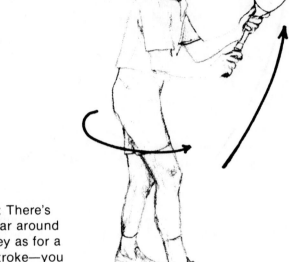

Figures 5.4, 5.5

Backhand volleying: There's no need to turn as far around for a backhand volley as for a backhand ground stroke—you don't need, or want, a big backswing.

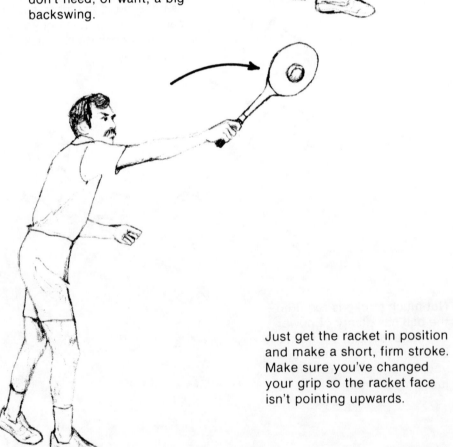

Just get the racket in position and make a short, firm stroke. Make sure you've changed your grip so the racket face isn't pointing upwards.

There are two critical shots to watch out for when you're volleying. The first is a shot straight at your head or body. It is almost impossible to make a decent return of a shot like that by trying to maneuver tne racket in front of your body. The only way to return that shot is to get out of its way, moving to the side of the ball and making either a forehand or backhand. One of the best ways for your opponent to break up a volley is to try to make you "eat a tennis ball for lunch," so be alert and ready to move quickly to the side.

The second dangerous shot is the attempted "pass shot." Your opponent will try either to get you away from the net or to score a point against you by using the back-court area behind you where you are vulnerable. He may either try to shoot a hard return past you—perhaps a volley of his own—just out of your reach, or he may send you a high lob over your head. The only way to defend against these shots is to be alert to the possibility that they will come and ready to run quickly backward or to a weak side. Don't be standing flat-footed at the net during volleying; keep your weight balanced on the balls of your feet, and be ready to move in any direction as fast as you can.

Practice the volley with a friend. Have him stand in mid-court, hitting a variety of shots to you, while you stand close to the net and volley them back. Be sure your friend hits you a few shots of every kind you're likely to see in a match—forehands, backhands, overheads, shots straight at the body, and pass shots. How well you volley depends entirely on how quick you are. People with naturally quick reactions learn the volley right away and rapidly learn how to place return shots with precision. People who are less quick will have trouble mastering the volley, no matter how much they practice. But do practice it at first, by all means, if only to find out whether net play is going to be one of your strong points or a weakness you should try to avoid. Don't ignore it, because like it or not you will have to volley occasionally in a match.

The lob

Like the volley, the lob is very uncomplicated; there isn't much form involved. There are two general kinds of lobs: a very high, underhand hit and a slicing hit.

The only trick in making the lob is to keep from letting your opponent know too early what's coming. Generally, approach the ball for a lob the way you would for a ground stroke, getting into position, pivoting and stepping, and shifting your weight as you make your backswing.

If the ball is coming at you relatively slowly and with a high bounce—say, chest-high or so—you can come under the ball with a fairly solid hit almost straight up. Make a normal backswing, but instead of stroking the ball straight through,

Figure 5.6

For a high lob, you should make a normal ground stroke, except that you must make a low, scooping stroke. Get the ball up as high as you can, without hitting it out of bounds.

make a deep arc and hit the ball at a sharp upward angle. (Figure 5.6.) The follow-through should continue up high, following the angle of the ball, and back over your shoulder. Don't put too much power on the ball—somewhat less than you would for a normal ground stroke. And be sure to hit it up at a very steep, nearly vertical angle; otherwise, you risk sending the ball far over the base line, out of bounds.

For a slicing lob, you should make a normal forehand or backhand shot, with a straight-ahead stroke, except that you turn the racket face up until it is about 30 degrees from the horizontal. (Figure 5.7.) When you stroke "through" the ball, it will fly up rather softly at a steep angle. Don't try to hit the ball very hard. The power in this stroke should be less than that of an ordinary ground stroke.

Figure 5.7

For the slice lob, a "surprise" shot, make a normal straight-through ground stroke, but with the racket face turned up—but not too far up, or the ball won't even go over the net, and will lose all power.

Figures 5.8, 5.9

The smash is the same motion you use for the serving stroke—a straight overhead shot, with the racket arm fully extended at point of contact.

Hit the ball strongly downward, but don't try to "kill" it. Use the smash sparingly.

The smash

The name of this stroke pretty accurately describes how you hit it. The smash is a "put away" stroke. As with the other two mentioned in this chapter, there's not much form to it.

The overhand motion of the smash is exactly like that of a serve, and you should try to hit it at least as hard as a good serve. The stroke is used only to return lobs or high-bouncing balls, high enough so that the contact is almost straight overhead, as high as the racket and arm fully extended. (Figures 5.8, 5.9.)

To return both lobs and high-bouncing balls, get into position well ahead of time and carefully keep your eye on the ball—a direct contact, in the center of the strings, is critical here. Make a backswing like that of a serve, with your arm bent and the racket behind you all the way, pointing down your back, and wait in that position until the ball reaches the right height for the stroke. Remember to hit the ball slightly downward, or you'll send it straight across to bounce off the back fence.

It's very important to make sure you're hitting the smash from high overhead and downward at a relatively steep angle. Because you're hitting the ball so hard, your accuracy is greatly reduced, and it is very easy to hit the ball out of bounds or into the net unless the angle of the shot is steep. Don't try to turn an ordinary shot the height of a ground stroke into a smash. If the ball is less than a foot or two above your head at the contact point, you shouldn't try to smash it.

The best advice on the smash is to avoid it except under the most ideal circumstances; it is rarely necessary to use it.

Photograph by Arthur Shay

6
Strategy

The more you master the fundamentals, the more you'll realize that tennis is as much a game of strategy as it is one of athletic skill. There are only a few basic strategies, but they can be applied in a vast number of ways—which gives the game its infinite variety. Many top players are so good at manipulating the basic strategies that they turn the game into an art form. Their performance drives home the point that using your head is as essential to winning in tennis as using your backhand. No matter how well you learn the strokes, unless you also learn the strategies of tennis you will always be playing a defensive game.

Strategy principles

The two key words in tennis strategy are *position* and *placement*. Position refers to where you or your opponent is standing in the court during a shot. Placement refers to hitting the ball to a particular spot in the opposite court.

75

From the defensive point of view, your opponent will attempt to move you into positions that will make it impossible for you to cover one part of the court; then he'll try to place the ball in that uncovered section. Offensively, you will be trying to do the same to him, by manipulating your own position on the court.

The basic rules of tennis strategy are:

1. Play your opponent deep.
2. Keep him moving.
3. Get up to the net when it's appropriate.

You should always try to keep your opponent deep, because that will limit the kinds of returns he can make. From a deep position he will have a narrower angle of possible shots he can make to you than if he were up close. And playing him deep will keep the ball on his side of the net longer, permitting you more time to get ready for his returns.

If you keep your opponent moving from side to side, you will reduce his ability to get into position and place his returns aggressively. If you continually keep him running off court to make his returns, chances are you'll eventually be able to put one completely out of his reach. For example, if he just dashed off the left side of the court to return your cross-court shot, it should be nearly impossible for him to get back and return your next shot if it is straight down the right sideline.

Finally, you should try to get up to the net whenever you can do so safely. This is the single most important offensive strategy in tennis, for two reasons. First, and more important, the closer you are to the net, the wider the angle of potential shots you can make (it is as if your opponent suddenly had twice as big an area to cover). Second, the closer you are to the net, the less time the ball will be in your court—meaning your opponent will have less time to

Possible shot angles: Deep play and net play

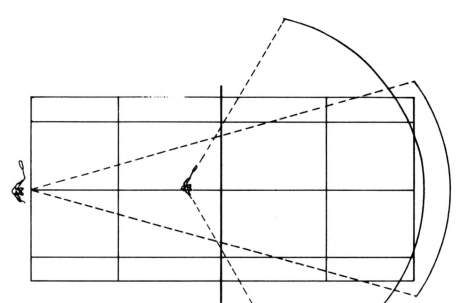

Figure 6.1

At the net, you have a far greater choice of shot angles than you do from the back court; for example, if you're at the net and your opponent is in the back court, you can make him run much farther to make his returns. That's why getting up to the net is such a deadly offensive maneuver.

recover and set himself for the return. (Figure 6.1.) If you're at the net, you can volley your shots, eliminating the time required for the bounce on your side and permitting you to make shots that are too quick to return. Getting to the net safely (without losing the point to a well-placed pass shot from your opponent) isn't easy and should be done cautiously—but once you're there, unless you make an error, you've almost got the point in the bag.

Elementary singles strategy

For normal groundstroke play, your position should be at least a foot or two behind the base line, and possibly farther back. For volleying, play no farther back than the service-court line, but no closer than will permit you to cover all your opponent's returns, depending on where he is on the court. Don't try to position yourself between the service-court line and the base line. That's "no-man's land," since the balls will bounce in that area, right at your feet, and will be very difficult to return. (Figure 6.2.) Except when you're volleying at the net, don't play any closer than necessary, since you'll find it easier to run forward to make a shot than to run backward.

Playing position and No-Man's Land

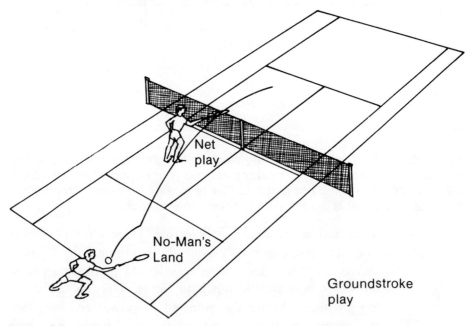

Net play

No-Man's Land

Groundstroke play

Figure 6.2

Avoid being in "no-man's land," the area between the baseline and the serving court line. That's where most balls are likely to bounce—and they'll be right at your feet.

During groundstroke rallies, your court position will be governed by what kind of shot your opponent makes, and from what position he makes it. For example, if you hit cross-court to his backhand, chances are his return will be a cross-court shot, particularly if he has to run to make the shot. Your best position, therefore, will be slightly across the center line from your opponent. If, however, you have hit cross-court to his forehand, he is more likely to return the ball straight down the line; so your best bet will be to position yourself on the same side of the center line as your opponent is on. (Figure 6.3.)

Cross-court shots

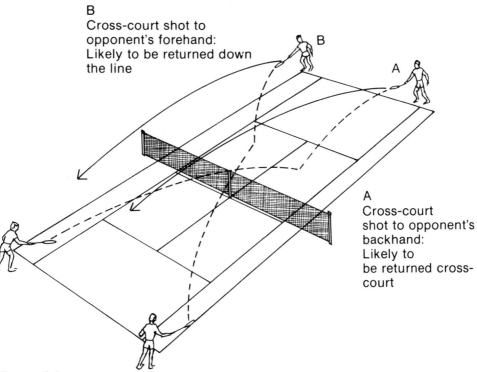

B
Cross-court shot to opponent's forehand: Likely to be returned down the line

A
Cross-court shot to opponent's backhand: Likely to be returned cross-court

Figure 6.3

A cross-court shot to your opponent's backhand is likely to be returned cross-court, too; while a cross-court shot to your opponent's forehand is more likely to be returned "down the line."

If possible, during groundstroke rallies you should try to place your shots deep, from one side to the other, waiting for your opponent to make a weak return that will let you move up to the net for the kill. If his ground game is solid and he is playing well back for your deep strokes, try a soft "drop shot" just over the net—but be careful. Drop shots should be used sparingly and cautiously, when you're sure they can't be returned, since you don't want to give your opponent a golden opportunity to come up to the net himself.

When you think the time is right to move up to the net, you will have to go in behind a good approach shot. This should be a good deep shot, but not too hard, that will give you time to move in and get set for a volley while your opponent is running to return your last shot. Don't try an approach shot if your opponent is in good court position and ready for a careful return, or he may send you either a quick pass shot when you are most vulnerable, still running in toward the net, or a lob over your head. Once you've decided to attack the net, be sure to follow your approach shot in—that is, run in on the same path with the ball. That gives you the best chance to handle your opponent's return from either side.

Once you're at the net, the basic idea is to hit your strokes downward and force your opponent to hit his strokes upward. Aim your shots at his feet or very sharply across the court, as close to parallel with the net as possible. Those are the most difficult shots to return.

Your opponent may try to drive you back with a lob, so watch him as he prepares to make his returns: if he begins a low, up-curving stroke or a slanted, chopping slice, you'll know he is about to send you a lob. If it is a relatively soft lob, you may be able to back up somewhat and hit the ball in the air, before the bounce—this, in fact, is the most likely occasion for a devastating overhead smash. If it is a very high, booming lob, you'll have to turn and run back as far as necessary, to a point well in back of the ball, and wait for it to bounce before you return it. (Timing your stroke to hit a high lob before it bounces is very difficult, since the ball is falling rapidly by the time it reaches a good height for hitting.)

If your opponent is trying to rush the net against you, watch out for his approach shot and return it as quickly as possible, hitting it as soon after the bounce as you can. You should try to get the ball back across the net while he is still crossing the no-man's land—too close in to cover the back court, but too far back to volley his shots.

If your opponent does successfully make it to the net, you have an option: try hitting pass shots—fast shots cross-court are the best—at as low an angle and from as close to the net as possible (this will reduce his maneuverability and force him to hit the ball up); or try a high lob over his head. On the other hand, if his net game is not particularly quick, you can try sending a hot return straight at his body, which he may handle poorly, allowing you a good chance at a quick pass shot on your next return.

Elementary doubles strategy

Playing a strategy game in doubles is much more difficult than in singles, since the key to strategy is forcing your opponent to leave some portion of his court uncovered, and then to hit to that vulnerable spot. In doubles, with two players on the court it is much less likely than in singles that any area will be left uncovered—despite the added nine feet of width in the alleys. In a groundstroke doubles game against reasonably careful players, it will be almost impossible for you to force your opponents into vulnerable positions either with placed shots or with hard, deep power shots. Consequently, the net game is even more important in doubles than in singles.

Normally, both serving and receiving teams will play with one man deep and one man short, either on opposite sides of the center line in basic fashion or on the same side of the center line, in "Australian" fashion. But it is quite possible—and even highly desirable—for both partners to rush the net whenever they can. It can be difficult to get both partners up to the net, but it is worth trying, since two men at the net present an almost invulnerable offense.

Naturally, the general principles of singles strategy apply to doubles as well, but there are some added nuances. For example, serving strategy becomes more important. In doubles, you should try to serve to your opponent's backhand whenever possible. His backhand shots are more likely to fall within the volleying range of your net man, who would then be able to place his return past the opposing net man, and perhaps allow you, the server, to rush the net. If your net man can't handle the return, your opponent's backhand return of your serve is more likely to fall within your own range.

The net man's most crucial defensive responsibility is to guard the alley opposite the back-court player—the weakest spot in the doubles court. It takes good teamwork between doubles partners to determine when the net man should try to return attempted pass shots, and when he should let the back-court man return them.

A useful doubles strategy is to have the net man "poach" serve returns. If you've hit a good, strong serve, your opponent will probably return the ball cross-court, attempting to hit the ball deep enough to give him time to get into rallying position. But if your net man quickly volleys a ball intended for you (the deep man), it will surprise your opponents and catch them unprepared, allowing you to make an approach shot on your next return and put both partners at the net.

When both partners are at the net, your opponents' only form of defense will be to send high lobs over your heads. The deep man, therefore, should play no closer than 10 or 15 feet from the net, ready to move back quickly for lobs.

Defensively, your opponents' net man presents your biggest threat, so you should attempt to neutralize him by sending as many high floaters over his head as you can during a rally. The net man won't be able to move back for them, and they will sometimes give you an opportunity to force the opposing back-court man into a vulnerable position, with an unprotected corner just waiting for a fast cross-court shot.

The normal position for partners who have the serve is for the server to stand midway between the center mark and the inside (singles) court sideline, behind the base line, while his partner stands next to the opposite alley line, midway between the net and the service-court line. (Figure 6.4.) For

Doubles playing position

A—Server's position
B—Serving partner
C—Receiving deep man

D—Receiving net man
E—Server's partner in "Australian" position

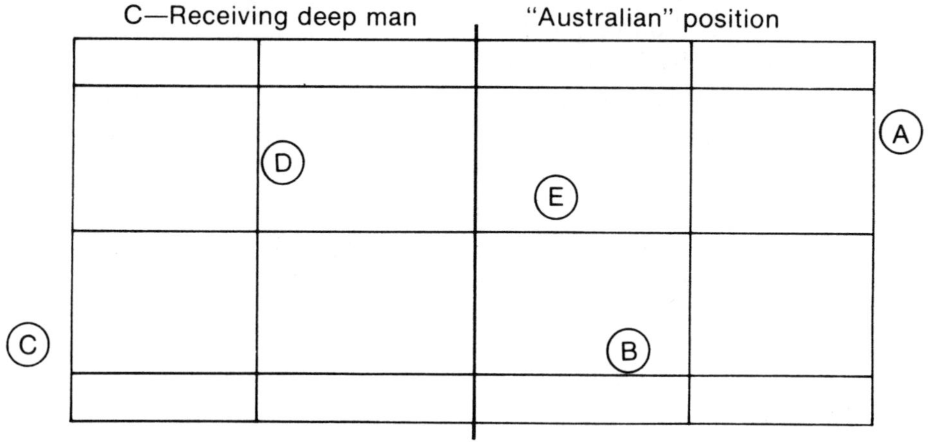

Figure 6.4

For doubles play, each team should have one man back and one man close to the net or at it. In standard doubles, the server's partner stands on the opposite side of the court from the server; in "Australian position," both server and his partner stand on the same side.

receiving partners, the deep man (receiver of the serve) should stand in essentially the same place as if he were serving (though a few feet farther back), and his partner should stand on the other side of the center line, roughly on the service-court line and midway between the center line and the alley. More advanced players, when serving, might want to try the "Australian" position. In this case the server's net man stands on his partner's side of the center line, though very close to the center. The better you get, the closer you should play to the net; when both players rush the net, however, they should stay about 15 feet away from it to defend against lobs.

Strategy situations

Here are some examples of situations you're likely to find yourself in during a match, and how you should react to them:

1. You've just hit a deep cross-court shot to your opponent's backhand, which he has had to run after. YOU SHOULD expect a cross-court shot back in the same direction; wait for it slightly to that side of the center line, several feet behind the base line.

2. Your opponent has had to race out of bounds to make his return on a forehand shot. YOU SHOULD hit the ball as far to his backhand side as possible.

3. Your opponent has just hit you a relatively soft, short shot and is backpedaling furiously in anticipation of your return. YOU SHOULD hit a very soft "drop shot" just over the net OR make a slow, deep approach shot across the center of the net and rush in behind it toward the net.

4. Your own soft return has given your opponent a good approach shot, cross-court to your forehand, and he is now rushing the net behind the shot. YOU SHOULD send a hard pass shot right up your forehand sideline OR slice a lob over his head and then get to the rear center of the court to await his return.

5. In doubles, your partner has just hit a deep serve, and your opponents' back-court man is about to make a backhand return straight across the center of the court. YOU SHOULD consider "poaching" the shot, hitting it down and away from the opposing net man.

6. In doubles, you, as deep man, realize your opponents are trying to set up an approach shot that will allow them to rush the net. YOU SHOULD hit high floaters over the head of the opposing net man.

7
Rules of the game

The governing body for tennis in the United States is the U.S. Lawn Tennis Association (USLTA). The international rule-making body, the International Lawn Tennis Federation, of which the USLTA is a member, is headquartered in London.

Starting to play

Players stand on opposite sides of the net; the one who hits the ball into play first is the server. In singles play, the court is 27 feet wide, marked by the inside lines of the "alleys" on the court. In doubles, the court is 36 feet wide, marked by the outside lines of the alleys. (Figure 7.1.)

Opponents usually choose sides and determine who will serve first by spinning a racket, with one player calling a side of the racket that has some identifying feature, such as lettering or numbers. Either the winner can choose the serve, in which case his opponent can choose the side he wants to play on, or he can choose sides, and the opponent can choose whether he wants to serve or not.

Court Dimensions

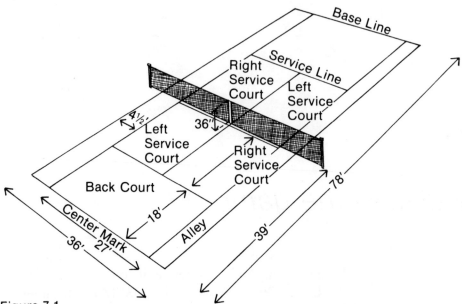

Figure 7.1

The standard tennis court dimensions.

During a set, players change sides whenever the number of games played is an odd number—that is, you change sides after the first game, the third game, the fifth game, and so on.

The serve

The server delivers the ball from behind the base line and from the appropriate side of the center mark, to the service court on the opposite side. The ball must bounce inside the opposite service court. (The same service boundaries apply for both singles and doubles; alleys are out of bounds on the serve.) The server hits his first ball from behind his right-hand court into the opposite court, and on the next point serves from the left side, switching back and forth after each point.

On each point, the server gets two chances to serve the ball properly. If his first serve is "good," that ball is played until one side scores a point. If, however, the server fails to hit the first ball into the proper service court; if he swings at the ball and misses; if the ball hits his partner or any permanent fixture on the court (other than the net); or if he commits a "foot fault," the serve is called a fault. He does not lose the point, but he has only one serve left. If the second serve also is a fault, the player has committed a "double fault," and he loses the point.

If the ball touches the net or strap but goes over and into the right court, the serve is called a let. The server gets to try it over again without losing one of his two serves. If his opponent attempts to hit the ball, however, the serve is considered good.

A "foot fault" is a serving fault called when the server's foot touches or crosses over the base line before he hits the ball, if he runs during the serve or changes position, or if he crosses the center mark before the ball is hit. A player can jump into the air during a serve, as long as neither foot touches the base line or any point inside it before the ball is hit.

If the serve—or any ball, for that matter, during a match—bounces on a line, it is considered in bounds and must be played.

After each game, the serve changes, and the server becomes the receiver. This is true in doubles, too: when one game is finished and the opponents take the serve, the player who has just finished serving will receive the first serve from the opponents.

During the game

Once the ball has been properly served to the correct service court, it may be returned to any part of the court (inside the alleys in singles, or including the alleys in doubles).

A player loses a point if the ball bounces more than once in his court; if he returns the ball so that when it bounces it is out of bounds (neither on nor within the lines of his opponent's court); if he hits the ball more than once (in doubles, the ball can be hit by only one partner); or if he returns the ball so that it hits or bounces off anything outside the court boundaries other than the net. If the return hits the net but goes over and bounces fair it is considered good and—unlike a "let" serve—must be played.

The player also loses the point if he volleys the ball before it crosses over the net; if his racket or hand or anything else within his control touches the ground inside his opponent's court; if he throws his racket at the ball (a careless or angry player might do so); or if he does anything deliberately to hinder his opponent's stroke at the ball.

If a player volleys a ball (hits it before it bounces) and his return is no good, he loses the point even if he was standing outside the court when he made the return and the ball would clearly have been out of bounds had he let it go.

Doubles play

In doubles, the teams choose sides and serve as in singles, but each pair of partners must decide between themselves in advance who shall serve and receive first, and must keep that order for each set.

Receiving partners keep to the same half, right or left, of their court throughout the set, while serving partners switch sides on each serve. That is, if you are receiving on the right-hand court, you remain in the right-hand court throughout the game. You would receive the first serve from your opponents, the third serve, the fifth serve, and so on. If you are serving in doubles, however, you keep the serve throughout one game, switching sides after each point just as in singles. The next time your side gets the serve, your partner serves the whole game, starting from the right-hand side.

Here's an example of how a doubles match would be played. You and your partner win the toss and choose to serve first; your opponents pick the court in which they would like to receive first, and choose which side of their court each one will play.

You serve the first game. You start the game by making the first serve from the right-hand side diagonally across the court to your opponent on the opposite side. After that point, you serve from the left-hand side and your partner moves over to the right; your opponents, however, stay in the same position, so you'll be serving to a different receiver on the second point.

After the first game is completed, you switch sides with your opponents and receive the first serve from your opponents from the right hand court. You and your partner each receive every other serve in every other game—game two, game four, and so on. After the first point, your opponents will switch and the server will serve to your partner, while you remain in the right-hand court. After the second game, you'll play a third game—with your partner serving the whole game this time—from the same side of the net as in the second game. For the fourth game, you switch sides with your opponents again, and so on.

Scoring

Tennis competition is scored in games, sets, and matches. To win a game, you must win at least four points and at least two more than your opponent. To win a set, you must win at least six games and at least two more games than your opponent. To win a match, you must win two out of three sets. In top-level tournament play, doubles partners and men playing singles usually must win three out of five sets; women must win two out of three.

Traditionally, game scores are called as follows:

No points: Love (from the French *l'oeuf,* or "egg," meaning "zero")

One point: 15

Two points: 30

Three points: 40

Four or more points: Game, deuce, ad in, or ad out. These are explained in the following paragraphs, but basically the score depends on whether you have won by two points, are tied with your opponent, are one point ahead of him, or are one point behind him.

There's neither rhyme nor reason in this unnecessarily complicated scoring system, but it has always been used and probably always will be.

When you have won four points, and your opponent has won no more than two, you have won the game. When you have won four points, but your opponent has won three, the score is called an advantage, or "ad." If the server is one point ahead, it's called ad in. If the receiver is one point ahead, it's called ad out. If you have won four points, and your opponent has won four points, the score is called deuce. You must keep playing until one of you has two more points than the other to win the game—no matter how many points it takes.

Here's an example of how a game would be scored:

You're serving, and you win the first point. The score you call out (the server calls the score, and always calls his score first, no matter whether he's ahead or behind) would be 15–love.

You win the second point. The score is now 30–love.

Your opponent wins the third point. The score is 30–15.

Your opponent wins the fourth point. The score is 30 all, meaning the game is tied so far.

You win the next point. The score is 40–30. (If you were to win the point after this as well, you would win the game.)

Your opponent wins the next point. The score is deuce.

Your opponent wins the next point. The score is ad out. (Remember, you are serving.)

You win the next point. Score: deuce again.

You win the point. Score: ad in.

You win the next point, and it's your game. The set score is now 1-0, although the minute your opponent takes over the serve, it becomes 0-1, since the server's score is always called first.

To win the set, you must win six games, but also at least two more games than your opponent has won. Therefore, if you've won six games and your opponent has won four, you win the set. If you've won six games but your opponent has won five, you play another game—if you win, the set is yours, 7-5; if you lose, the set score is 6-6, and you will have to play at least two more games.

Games can go on endlessly, and so can sets, unless you decide in advance to play a tie breaker at some point—which most players decide will be after both players have won six games each. Rules of the USLTA specify a nine-point tie breaker as follows:

After the set score has reached 6 all, the next regular server serves two points, the first from the right-hand court and the second from the left-hand court. His opponent then does the same, serving two more points; and then the two change sides and repeat the process.

Play continues until one player has won five points and is declared the winner of the set, with a score of 7-6. If after eight serves the score is tied 4 all, then the player who served the last point makes one more serve. Whoever wins that point, the ninth point, wins the tie breaker and the set at 7-6.

The procedure for a doubles tie breaker is exactly the same, with one additional wrinkle: you serve two points, one of your opponents serves two, your partner serves two, and the other opponent serves two. For the ninth point, the last player to serve makes the set-deciding serve.

Many times, when play on one point has been long and

arduous, the server can forget which side he should serve the next ball from. He can figure that out easily from the score. The serve for any game always starts from the right-hand court; so whenever the points won by both sides total an even number, the server should be serving from the right-hand court. When the total of points made is an odd number, he should be serving from the left-hand court.

When a game goes on and on, then, the score will be deuce when the server delivers from the right side, and advantage (either in or out) when he serves from the left side. Therefore, the right-hand court is traditionally called the deuce court, and the left-hand court is called the ad court.

Glossary

Ace—a serve that lands fair but which the receiver fails even to touch with his racket.

Ad—short for *advantage;* the first point scored after deuce. If the server makes the point, it is "ad in." If the receiver makes the point, it is "ad out."

Ad Court—the left-hand side of the court.

All—an even score, such as 30 all in a game, or 6 all in a set.

Alley—the 4½-foot-wide area on either side of the singles court that marks off the wider doubles court.

Angle Shot—a ball hit at an extreme angle across the court.

Approach Shot—a return made so the player can run up to the net for volleying.

Back Court—the rear half of the court, from the service-court line to the base line.

Backhand—a stroke that requires the player to bring the racket across his body; for right-handed players, a stroke made on the left side.

Backhand Court—for right-handed players, the left side of the court; for left-handed players, the right side.

Backswing—the motion involved in bringing the racket backward to build up power for the stroke.

Base Line—the back boundary of the tennis court, 39 feet from the net.

Break Service—to win a game in which your opponent has the serve.

Cannonball—a very hard, flat serve.

Center Mark—the short mark in the base line that divides the court in half for serving.

Center Service Line—the line perpendicular to the net that divides the two service courts.

Center Strap—a strap in the center of the net that holds the net down at a height of 36 inches.

Closed Face—the face of the racket when turned slightly downward, the strings at less than a 90-degree angle to the ground.

Cross-Court Shot—a ball hit diagonally over the net, from one corner to the opposite corner on the other side of the net.

Deep Shot—a ball that bounces near the base line.

Deuce—a tied game when each player has three points or more.

Deuce Court—the right-hand side of the court.

Double Fault—when the server fails to make a good serve on both his chances. A point for the receiver.

Doubles—a match with a team of two players on each side of the net.

Drive—a hard, offensive shot.

Drop Shot—a ball hit very softly that just barely goes over the net.

Drop Volley—a drop shot hit on a volley.

Fast Court—a court with a smooth, hard surface that allows the ball to bounce fast and low.

Fault—a bad serve.

Foot Fault—a fault caused when the player crosses the base line with one or both feet, moves improperly, or crosses over the center mark before the serve is hit.

Forecourt—area between the net and the service court line.

Forehand—a stroke made on the same side of the body as the racket arm.

Forehand Court—the right side of the court for right-handed players; the left side for left-handed players.

Frame—the oval part of the racket holding the strings.

Game—when one player wins at least four points and at least two points more than his opponent.

Grip—the method of holding the racket; also, the leather or rubber covering on the racket handle.

Ground Strokes—strokes made after the ball has bounced, hit relatively straight across the net.

Gut—racket strings made from sheep or hog intestines.

Half Volley—to hit the ball immediately after it bounces.

Head—the frame and strings of the racket.

Hold Serve—for the server, to win a game he is serving.

Kill—to smash the ball very hard.

Let—a serve that hits the top of the net but is otherwise good; the serve is delivered again, unless the opponent moves to return it.

Lob—a ball hit very high into the air, usually far enough to pass over the head of any opponent at the net.

Love—zero; no score.

Love Game—a game in which one player wins four points in a row, but his opponent wins none.

Love Set—a set in which one player wins six games in a row, but his opponent wins none.

Match—generally, a match is complete when one player wins two sets out of three; for doubles or for men's championship matches, the winner must take three sets out of five.

Match Point—the single point that can win a match for one side.

Mid-Court—the general area in the center of the playing court, midway between the net and base line, in the area of the service-court line.

Net Game—volleying play with at least one player close to the net.

Net Man—in doubles, the partner who plays closest to the net.

No-Man's Land—the mid-court area where the ball often bounces near the player's feet, making returns difficult.

Open Face—the racket face turned slightly up, with the angle of the strings (from the net side of the racket to the ground) at more than 90 degrees.

Opening—a good chance for a player to score an easy point as a result of an opponent's strategic mistake.

Out—a ball landing outside the playing court.

Pass Shot—a ball hit out of the reach of a net player.

Percentage Tennis—a conservative style of tennis playing that frowns on risky, aggressive tactics and favors reducing basic playing errors.

Place—to hit the ball to a specific spot in the opponent's court.

Press—a wooden frame bolted tight to a wooden racket face when the racket is not in use, to keep it from warping.

Rally—back-and-forth play after the serve.

Round Robin—a tournament in which each player plays every other player.

Rush—advance to the net after hitting an approach shot.

Seed—ranking; an arrangement of players in tournament matches so that the most favored players don't play together until the last round.

Serve, or Service—the hit that puts the ball into play, for each point of a game.

Service-Court Line—the line parallel to the net and 21 feet from it that marks the back of the service court and is the farthest point at which the serve may bounce.

Set—completion of a series of games, determined when one player has won at least six games and at least two more than his opponent (except in the case of a tie breaker, in which the final game score of the set is 7-6).

Set Point—the single point that can win a set for one player.

Singles—a contest between two players.

Slice—a sharp downward stroke at the ball on the return, giving it backspin.

Slow Court—a court with a rough surface that makes the ball bounce slower and higher than on other courts.

Smash—a very hard overhead shot, hit downward into the opponent's court as a "put-away" shot.

Spin—rotation of the ball in flight after it is hit at an angle; results in erratic bounces that can make the return difficult.

Straight Sets—to win a match without losing a set.

Tape—the canvas band that runs along the length of the top of the net.

Tennis Elbow—a painful swelling in the elbow joint of the racket arm, usually caused by constant overextension of the arm.

Throat—the part of the racket between the head and the handle.

Tie Breaker—a nine-point series played to decide the winner of a set when the score is tied at 6 all.

Trajectory—the angle or curvature of the flight of the ball.

Volley—to return the ball before it bounces.

Wood Shot—a ball hit by the racket frame instead of the strings.

Index